Gattaca

Howard Mahmood

FADE IN

A white title appears on a black screen.

"As night-fall does not come at once, neither does oppression...It is in such twilight that we all must be aware of change in the air

- however slight - lest we become victims of the darkness."

Justice William O. Douglas

The title fades off, replaced by a second title.

"I not only think that we will tamper with

Mother Nature, I think Mother wants us to."

William Gaylin

The second title fades off, leaving a dark screen.

The darkness gradually gives way to a dawning light.

We are confronted with sight of a barren, empty landscape. A wide expanse of wasteland.

Suddenly, without warning, an elephant tusk falls from the sky and crashes onto the parched ground. The earth-shuddering impact causes the tusk to rebound once in slow motion before finally settling to the desert floor in a cloud of dust.

The first tusk is quickly followed by a second, also dropping from the heavens. It lands near the first. Another tusk smashes to earth several yards away. Yet another comes crashing into the foreground.

Finally the dust settles upon a graveyard of tusks.

DISSOLVE TO

A BARREN, EMPTY LANDSCAPE

In another region of the wasteland, a forest of tree trunks suddenly rains down from the sky. The trunks thump to the hard ground, also rebounding in slow motion. Cleanly sawn, branchless, palm-like trunks, they come to rest in the dust only to be followed by a second cascade of lumber.

When the dust finally clears. the felled tree trunks lie in a huge, log-jam in the desert.

DISSOLVE TO

A BARREN, EMPTY LANDSCAPE

Next to descend from the sky, a torrent of firewood. One shower after another, crashing to the plain. Enough chopped lumber to fuel a thousand hearths.

DISSOLVE TO

A BARREN, EMPTY LANDSCAPE

Joining the rest of the debris is a deluge of slate - sheets of shale from a great unseen quarry in the sky come slamming to earth. Some of the pieces shattering, some rebounding into the air until the granite litters acres of landscape as far as the eye can see.

TITLES ARE SPACED APPROPRIATELY THROUGHOUT THE PRECEDING

SEQUENCE. THE FINAL TITLE READS:

T H E N O T - T O O - D I S T A N T F U T U R E

The camera commences a long, slow pull-back from the pile of elephant tusks. Gradually they are revealed as human fingernails magnified many hundreds of times. The tree trunks are mere hair follicles. The firewood, whiskers. The slate, flakes of skin.

INT. INCINERATOR. EARLY MORNING.

A naked MAN, thirties, seen in profile, is crouched upon a metal floor inside a small, brushed stainless steel tank, rubbing his skin raw with a wire brush. JEROME MORROW.

Having completed his scrupulous ablutions, Jerome arches his lean frame through the small, oval door of the metal room with practised ease.

Securing the thick, fireproof windowed door behind himself, he turns a switch to release gas into the vacated chamber. The gas instantly ignites in what is now revealed to be a gleaming modern stainless-steel custom-made incinerator.

We refocus on a MAGNIFIED CLOSE UP of his exfoliated flesh in the incinerator as it blackens, curls and burns.

Jerone covers himself with a silk robe and steps into a pair of backless slippers.

INT. EUGENE'S CONDOMINIUM. EARLY MORNING.

JEROME emerges from the incinerator room into a large, luxurious loft-style condo containing a bizarre assortment of equipment - arranged somewhat like a production line.

Long, scrupulously clean metal work benches are arranged along one entire wall. Laid out on the benches in neat rows are dozens of plastic bags - some filled, some unfilled. Instruments on trays - various types of tweezers, scissors and other less familiar utensils. Round, stainless steel containers filled with hairs of differing lengths and other body matter.

JEROME approaches another man slumped over one of the benches.

EUGENE. He clutches an empty vodka bottle. He is snoring lightly - sleeping off the night before. As JEROME gently prises the bottle out of his hand, we are struck by the similarity of Eugene's face to Jerome's.

Jerome pulls Eugene's chair back from the desk with surprising ease. A wheelchair - a modern, ergonomic design. Jerome wheels

Eugene to a bedroom and, with some difficulty, hauls the larger man onto the bed. Through his alcoholic fog, Eugene feebly co- operates - his paralyzed legs a particular dead weight.

After covering Eugene with a blanket, Jerome enters a bathroom containing a surgically-clean stainless steel basin, sink, shower and toilet.

Beside the toilet stands a large, industrial-style stainless steel refrigerator.

Donning protective gloves, Jerome opens the liquid-nitrogen cooled refrigerator. A cloud of condensed water vapor billows out. Revealed inside the fridge are racks of labelled jars and silicon pouches - some containing a yellowish liquid, some a deep, red liquid.

In front of one of the jars is a handwritten shopping list -

"TRUFFLES, CIGS, VODKA". Jerome smiles to himself as he retrieves the note along with one of the jars. He checks the jar's label. Satisfied with the date written there, he breaks the seal and pours the contents into the clear, silicon pouch of an IV-like device lying on the steel bathroom counter.

He seals the pouch and checks the apparatus by opening the valve on its fine tube and squirting a small quantity of the liquid into the nearby toilet bowl, as one would test a syringe. We remain on Jerome's face as he reaches between his legs and inserts the pouch.

Reopening the refrigerator, Jerome slides out a tray containing neat rows of slim, fingertip-sized plastic sachets filled with a deep, red-colored liquid. He removes his gloves, selects one of the sachets and carefully adheres the sachet to the pad at the end of his index finger. He prepares a second sachet for his middle finger. Jerome then applies skin-colored cover-up makeup to the sachets, blending them in with the color of his fingers.

JEROME, still dressed in his robe, climbs a large, spiral staircase to the floor above.

INT. JEROME'S CONDOMINIUM. EARLY MORNING.
He emerges at the top of the staircase into a similarly large, loft-stlye condominium. Through the floor to ceiling window that opens onto a balcony we see that dawn is only just starting to leak into the night sky.

In the bedroom JEROME removes a shirt from a drycleaning bag.

Printed on the bag - "Confidentiality Guaranteed". He emerges from his bedroom, dressed in a smart albeit unconventionally cut suit. He adjusts his tie in the mirror, careful not to disturb the sachets attached to his fingertips.

INT. INVESTIGATOR'S POOL. MORNING.
A lone MAN swims a ferocious lap of freestyle in what appears to be a pool of enormous length - yet he never reaches the pool's end. We pull wider to reveal that the man is swimming against an artificial current in a pool barely larger than himself.

Abruptly, the man stops and stands up - the fast-flowing current instantly stilled. We glimpse the face of INVESTIGATOR LUCAS.

Thirties, he has a youthful yet rigid face. We have the impression that he does not swim for pleasure.

EXT. CONDOMINIUM COMPLEX. MORNING.
It is still early as JEROME exits the building's underground parking garage in an immaculate Studebaker Avanti and proceeds down the long straight driveway. He exchanges a wave with a
GARDENER trimming a lawn.
The whir of the car's electric powered engine belies its conventional appearance.

EXT. GATTACA AEROSPACE CORPORATION. DAY.
JEROME's car exits a highway and turns up the sweeping road leading to the parking lot of "GATTACA AEROSPACE CORPORATION".

A sleek, modern, low-rise industrial compound boasting perfectly manicured landscaped gardens.

INT. GATTACA AEROSPACE CORPORATION. DAY.

JEROME strides purposefully up to the entranceway with hundreds of other GATTACA EMPLOYEES. He carries himself with a certain arrogance, a cool detachment. All employees wear similarly unconventionally-cut suits, short coiffed hair and robust tans.

The Gattaca employees are a seemingly equal split of men and women and a diverse range of ethnicities.

They filter through a row of channels supervised by SECURITY GUARDS. Each channel contains a computerized security device, featuring a slim groove in which the employee places a finger under the watchful eye of a Security Guard.

Jerome gives a polite nod to a Guard as he places his index finger in the groove. His fingertip is jabbed with the finest of needles and a minute blood sample taken.

The blood specimen confirms Jerome's identity - an ID photograph appearing on a computer screen.

Out of the corner of his eye, Jerome spies a young woman entering through the adjacent channel. She is also sneaking a glance in his direction - IRENE. Catching each other looking, they both quickly avert their eyes.

As Jerome enters the computer facility of Gattaca Aerospace Corporation he furtively glances at the pin-prick puncture in his fingertip sachet.

SOMEWHERE IN DEEP SPACE.

A GATTACA spacecraft skirts an asteroid. Taking advantage of the rock's gravitational pull, the craft slingshots deeper into the black void. Then abruptly the craft and the asteroid freeze in mid-space, suddenly reverse direction and proceed forward again - the spacecraft taking a slightly adjusted course.

We pull back to reveal that the journey is merely a highly realistic graphic representation on a GATTACA computer screen operated by JEROME.

Appearing simultaneously alongside the computer animation is a seemingly never-ending column of computer instructions for this celestial navigation - the incomprehensible language of the computer programmer.

140 #x20x08x$$x20x08x$$x20x08x$$x20{
150 #x00x00x00x00x00x00x00x00x00x00
160 #xfexfexfexfexfexfexfexfexfexfe

Jerome is transported - plotting a path through the heavens.

As his fingers fly across the keys he does not once take his eyes from the screen.

His is one of hundreds of ergonomically designed work stations, arranged in ever-widening circles in a huge, curcular, well- appointed if antiseptic room. Each curved desk contains a computer terminal consisting of a keyboard and a slim, transparent screen behind which is seated a PROGRAMMER, designing software for the aerospace agency. At the center of the room is a donut-shaped command console, chairs facing outwards, from which operations are monitored.

Floor to ceiling smoked-glass curved walls offer the only concession to nature - a tinted view of a man-made, meticulously landscaped garden.

Jerome tears himself away from his screen and picks up a discreet mini-vac. He vacuums between the keys of his keyboard.

DIRECTOR JOSEF, 50's, a shorter, official-looking man approaches. His assistant IRENE stands at his shoulder.

DIRECTOR JOSEF
You keep your work station so clean, Jerome.

JEROME
--Next to Godliness, isn't that what they say?
The Director smiles at the notion and places a computer disc on Jerome's desk.

DIRECTOR JOSEF
I reviewed your flight plan. Not one error in a hundred thousand keystrokes. Phenomenal.
(placing a hand on Jerome's shoulder)
It's right that someone like you is taking us to the Belt.
(glancing to notification on Jerome's screen)
You have a substance test.
The Director briskly departs, Irene in tow. At a nearby work station, a painfully thin programmer, NAPOLEON, perks up at the mention of the test.
Jerome merely shrugs and pretends to reach down and scratch his ankle. However he surreptitiously produced one of Eugene's transparent specimen bags from his sock. An EXTREME CLOSE UP reveals the bag's contents - flakes of skin, hair follicles, eyelashes, a fingernail. Cupping the bag in his hand to avoid detection, Jerome sprinkles the fraudulent body matter over his keyboard, desk surfaces and the floor around his work station.
He opens his desk drawer and casually scatters the remainder of the bag. Finally he inspects a comb already laced with two hair follicles.
Jerome rises from his work station and makes his way towards the testing lab.

INT. GATTACA AEROSPACE CORPORATION - TESTING LABORATORY. DAY.
White-coated LAMAR, forties, buzzcut, a man's man, checks
JEROME's eyes with an instrument. Satisfied with his examination, he passes a transparent plastic container to
JEROME. Standing directly in front of the technician with his back to camera, Jerome opens his fly. A steady stream of urine begins to flow into the container from Jerome's hidden pouch.

LAMAR
(staring admiringly at the discharge)
Jerome...never shy. Pisses on command.
You've got a beautiful cock. I ever told you that, Jerome?

JEROME
(deadpan as he continues to urinate)
Only every time I'm in here.

Jerome hands the container to Lamara who seals and label it as
Jerome refastens his trousers.

LAMAR
I see a lot of cocks. I speak from experience.
Yours is a beautiful example. Why didn't my folks order a cock like that for me?
LAMAR pours the urine sample into a high-tech device where it is instantly analyzed.
The urine identifies Jerone while also registering a negative drug reading. The computer reads
"VALID".

LAMAR
(walking Jerome to the door)
If everything goes to plan, this could be the last time I see you for a while. One week to go. Please tell me you're the least bit excited.

JEROME
I'll tell you at the end of the week.
Jerome departs.

INT. GATTACA - RESTROOM. DAY.
JEROME enters the restroom and glances at the toilet stalls.
Only three in the bank of twenty is occupied. He tarries at the mirror above the uniform line of basins, unnecessarily reknotting his tie.
A toilet flushes and a COLLEAGUE exits one of the stalls. He and Jerome exchange a nod. When the man has exited the restroom,
Jerome enters the man's vacated stall.

INT. GATTACA - TOILET STALL. DAY.
JEROME immediately feels around the back of the toilet bowl and detaches a secreted stainless steel container.
With surprising swiftness and dexterity, Jerome removes an extremely fine contact lens from each eye and drops the pair into the toilet bowl. He inserts two replacement lenses from the container and reattaches it in its hiding place.
Jerome flushes the toilet and exits the stall. He checks in the mirror that his new contact lenses are properly inserted.

INT. GATTACA - CORRIDOR. DAY.
Walking back along one of the long, glass-walled corridors,
JEROME becomes aware of a peculiar noise in the complex - or to be more precise, a lack of noise. The incessant tapping of computer keys has stilled.
As Jerome gazes through the glass walled corridor, we see the reflection of his face, deep in thought.
JEROME (VO)
The most unremarkable of events. Jerome

Morrow, Navigator First class, is only days away from a one-year manned mission to 951
Gaspra in the Outer Asteroid Belt. Nothing so unique in that. Last year over one thousand citizens from every walk of life embarked on some space mission or other. Besides, selection for Jerome was virtually guaranteed at birth. He is blessed with all the physical and intellectual gifts required for such an arduous undertaking, a genetic quotient second to none.
Jerome's gaze drifts to the sky.
JEROME (VO)
No, there is truly nothing remarkable about the progress of Jerome Morrow, except that I am not Jerome Morrow.

EXT. BEACH. DUSK - THIRTY-ODD YEARS EARILER
A starry sky. The camera tilts down to find palm trees swaying against a setting sun.
JEROME (VO)
I was conceived in the Riviera. Not the
French Riviera.
The camera tilts down further to find a Buick Riviera parked in a deserted beachfront parking lot on a polluted stretch of beach.
JEROME (VO)
The Detroit variety.
Through the car's steamed windows we see Jerome's mother and father, MARIA and ANTONIO, early twenties, making love.
JEROME (VO)
They used to say that a child conceived in love, has a greater chance of happiness. They don't say that any more.

INT. FAMILY PLANNING CLINIC. DAY.
MARIA, wearing a medical gown, lies on an examining table, feet in stirrups. A NURSE, forties, wheels an instrument tray towards her. Maria suddenly disengages her feet from the stirrups and swings her legs off the table.

NURSE
What are you doing?

MARIA
(shaking her head)
I can't do this.

NURSE
(misinterpreting the problem)
I told you, the government pays. It's all taken care of.

MARIA
No, you don't understand. I can't.
The nurse places a comforting hand on Maria's shoulder.

NURSE
(reassuring)
The doctor will give you something.

MARIA
(removing the hand, adamant)
I'm not doing it.

NURSE
(trying to make her see reason)
Honey, you've made one mistake--
The remark stings Maria.

NURSE
(softening her tone)
--I've read your profile. I don't know about the father but you carry enough hereditary
factors on your own.
(pause)
You can have other children.

MARIA
(holding her swollen stomach protectively)
Not like this one.

NURSE
(trying to be diplomatic)
Honey, look around you. The world doesn't want one like that one.
Maria gets off the table and reaches for her clothes laying across a chair.

MARIA
(irate)
You don't know what it will be!
The nurse watches Maria as she dresses, genuinely bewildered.

NURSE
(calling out to Maria as she disappears out of the door)
The child won't thank you!

INT. DELIVERY ROOM. DAY.
We focus on a crucifix dangling on a rosary. Tilting up we find the rosary clasped
between MARIA and ANTONIO's intertwined hands.
JEROME (VO)
Those were early days--days when a priest could still persuade someone to put their
faith in God's hands rather than those of the local geneticist.
Bathed in sweat, Maria gives a final push on the delivery table.

While still attached to his umbilical cord, the heel of the
NEWBORN BABY BOY is immediately pricked by a masked NURSE. A minute drop
of blood is inserted into an analyzing machine.
Even as the baby is put into Maria's arms, page after page of data begins to appear on a
monitor, pulsing warning signals throughout the spreadsheets.
Two assisting NURSES exchange a look. Antonio senses something amiss.

ANTONIO
What's wrong?
JEROME (VO)
Of course, there was nothing wrong with me.
Not so long ago I would have been considered a perfectly healthy, normal baby. Ten
fingers, ten toes. That was all that used to matter.
But now my immediate well-being was not the sole concern.
Antonio turns his attention from his baby to the data appearing on the monitor. We see
individual items highlighted amongst the data - "NERVE CONDITION -
PROBABILITY 60%", "MANIC DEPRESSION -

42%", "OBESITY - 66%", "ATTENTION DEFICIT DISORDER - 89%"--
JEROME (VO)
My destiny was mapped out before me-- all my flaws, predispositions and
susceptibilities - most untreatable to this day. Only minutes old, the date and cause of
my death was already known.
Antonio focuses on a final highlighted item on the monitor's screen, "HEART
DISORDER - 99% - EARLY FATAL POTENTIAL.".
"LIFE EXPECTANCY - 33 YEARS".

NURSE
The name?
(typing details into birth certificate)
For the certificate.

MARIA
Antonio--

ANTONIO
(correcting her)
--No, Vincent Antonio.
With a computer stylus he signs the nurse's handheld screen.

EXT. TRACT HOME - BACKYARD. DAY.
2-YEAR-OLD JEROME (REFERRED TO BY HIS GIVEN NAME OF
"VINCENT"
FOR MOST OF THE FOLLOWING FLASHBACK) running with a toy rocket falls
more in clumsiness than fatigue. MARIA suddenly whisks up the toddler.

MARIA
(hysterical)
Oh, Vincent, Vincent, Vincent...I can't let you out of my sight.
Maria frantically listens to her young son's heartbeat. For his part, Vincent appears surprised by the attention. Maria places a portable oxygen mask over Vincent's mouth.
JEROME (VO)
I was born Vincent Antonio Luca. And from an early age I came to think of myself as others thought of me - chronically ill.
Every skinned knee and runny nose treated as if it were life-threatening.

INT. DAY CARE CENTER. DAY.
MARIA and ANTONIO drop off dark-haired 2-YEAR-OLD VINCENT at a
Day Care Center.
JEROME (VO)
And my parents soon realized that wherever
I went, my genetic prophecy preceded me.
While HEALTHY CHILDREN play outside on tricycles, clamber over jungle-gyms and finger-paint, the PRE-SCHOOL TEACHER shows
Vincent into a room where CHILDREN WITH OBVIOUS DISABILITIES sleep on mats.
Maria wheels around and marches out of the center with Vincent in her arms. Antonio follows close behind, pleading with his wife to see sense.
JEROME (VO)
They put off having any more children until they could afford not to gamble - to bring a child into the world in what has become the "natural" way.

EXT. HOME. DAY.
ANTONIO reluctantly shows off his spotless Buick Riviera to a prospective BUYER.
JEROME (VO)
It meant selling the beloved Buick.
The two men haggle over the price while MARIA, holding VINCENT in her arms, looks on. Finally money and a pink slip are exchanged.
VINCENT (VO)
My father got a good price. After all, the only accident he'd ever had in that car was me.
As the BUYER drives away, Antonio shrugs to Maria to hide his disappointment.

EXT. GENETIC COUNSELLING OFFICE BUILDING. DAY.
ANTONIO, MARIA and 2-YEAR-OLD VINCENT exit a packed commuter bus and enter a Genetic Counselling office building bearing the sign - "PRO-CREATION".

INT. GENETIC COUNSELLING OFFICE. DAY.
A GENETICIST stares into a high-powered microscope as ANTONIO,
MARIA and 2-YEAR-OLD VINCENT are shown into the office by a
NURSE. On the counter beside the Geneticist is a glass-doored industrial refrigerator containing petri dishes arranged on racks several feet high.

GENETICIST
(to the nurse, without taking his eyes from his binocular microscope)
Put up the dish.
While Antonio and Maria take a seat in front of a television monitor, the Nurse puts a labelled petri dish under a video- equipped microscope. The Geneticist swings around in his chair to greet his clients.
Four magnified clusters of cells - eight cells on each cluster
- appear on the television screen.

GENETICIST
Your extracted eggs...
(noting the couple's names from data along the edge of the screen)
...Maria, have been fertilized with...
Antonio's sperm and we have performed an analysis of the resulting pre-embryos.
After screening we're left with two healthy boys and two healthy girls. Naturally, no critical pre-dispositions to any of the major inheritable diseases. All that remains is to select the most compatible candidate.
Maria and Antonio exchange a nervous smile.

GENETICIST
First, we may as well decide on gender.
Have you given it any thought?

MARIA
(referring to the toddler on her knee)
We would like Vincent to have a brother... you know, to play with.
The Geneticist nods. He scans the data around the edge of the screen.

GENETICIST
You've already specified blue eyes, dark hair and fair skin. I have taken the liberty of eradicating any potentially prejudicial conditions - premature baldness, myopia, alcoholism and addictive susceptibility, propensity for violence and obesity--

MARIA
(interrupting, anxious)
--We didn't want--diseases, yes.

ANTONIO
(more diplomatic)
We were wondering if we should leave some things to chance.

GENETICIST
(reassuring)
You want to give your child the best possible start. Believe me, we have enough imperfection built-in already. Your child doesn't need any additional burdens. And keep in mind, this child is still you, simply the best of you.

You could conceive naturally a thousand times and never get such a result.

ANTONIO
(squeezing Maria's hand)
He's right, Maria. That's right.
Maria is only half-convinced, but the Geneticist swiftly moves on.

GENETICIST
Is there any reason you'd want a left-handed child?

ANTONIO
(blank)
Er, no...

GENETICIST
(explaining)
Some believe it is associated with creativity, although there's no evidence. Also for sports like baseball it can be an advantage.

ANTONIO
(shrugs)
I like football.

GENETICIST
(injecting a note of levity)
I have to warn you, Mr Luca, he's going to be at least a head taller than you.
Prepare for a crick in the neck in sixteen years time.
Antonio beams proudly.

GENETICIST
(scanning the data on the screen)
Anything I've forgotten?

MARIA
(hesitant about broaching the subject)
We want him--we were hoping he would get married and have children. We'd like grandchildren.

GENETICIST
(conspiratorial smile)
I understand. That's already been taken care of.
(an afterthought)
Now you appreciate I can only work with the raw material I have at my disposal but for a little extra...I could also attempt to insert sequences associated with enhanced mathematical or musical ability.

MARIA
(suddenly enthused)
Antonio, the choir...

GENETICIST
(interjecting, covering himself)
I have to caution you it's not fool-proof.
With multi-gene traits there can be no guarantees.

ANTONIO
How much extra?

GENETICIST
It would be five thousand more.
Antonio's face falls.

ANTONIO
I'm sorry, there's no way we can.

GENETICIST
Don't worry. You'll probably do just as well singing to him in the womb.
(rising to end the appointment)
We can implant the most successful pre-embryo tomorrow afternoon.
Maria is staring at the four magnified clumps on the screen.

MARIA
What will happen to the others?

GENETICIST
(reassuring)
They are not babies, Maria, merely
"human possibilities".
Removing the petri dish from beneath the lens of the microscope, he points out the four
minuscule specks.

GENETICIST
Smaller than a grain of sand.

DISSOLVE TO
INT. TRACT HOME. DAY.
A red pencil draws a mark on a doorway at the height of a child's head. The child moves
away and the name, "ANTON 11" is written beside the mark by proud father,
ANTONIO.
JEROME (VO)
That's how my brother, Anton, came into the world - a son my father considered worthy
of his name.

There is little physical similarity between 11-YEAR-OLD ANTON and 13-YEAR-OLD VINCENT standing beside him, apart from their height. In fact Vincent is mortified to see that his younger brother's mark is a fraction of an inch higher than the mark beside his own name, "VINCENT 13". Vincent runs from the room.

EXT. BEACH. DAY.
13-YEAR-OLD VINCENT and 11-YEAR-OLD ANTON sit together on a windswept beach.
Anton picks up a broken shell and deliberately slices the tip of his thumb with the sharp edge. He hands the shell to Vincent who hesitantly follows suit.
JEROME (VO)
By the time we were playing at blood brothers I understood that there was something very different flowing through my veins.
The two brothers press their thumbs together, merging the blood.
JEROME (VO)
And I'd need an awful lot more than a drop if I was going to get anywhere.

EXT. BEACH. LATER IN THE DAY.
While ANTONIO and MARIA doze under a beach umbrella, ANTON and
VINCENT enter the water, diving through the waves. From above we watch their two young bodies swimming beside each other beyond the breakers.
JEROME (VO)
Our favorite game was "chicken". When our parents weren't watching, we used to swim outside the flags, as far out as we dared. It was about who would get scared and turn back first.
Suddenly VINCENT stops swimming, pulling up sharply in the water, exhausted and fearful. He watches ANTON swim on into the distance.
JEROME (VO)
Of course, it was always me. Anton was by far the stronger swimmer and he had no excuse to fail.

INT. SCHOOL - CLASSROOM. DAY.
A TEACHER gives a physics lesson. The bespectacled 13-YEAR-OLD
VINCENT has his arm energetically raised at each opportunity but is never called upon. Eventually he lowers his arm in defeat.
JEROME (VO)
My genetic scarlet letter continued to follow me from school to school. When you're told you're prone to learning disabilities, it's sometimes easier not to disappoint anybody.

EXT. STREET. NIGHT.
13-YEAR-OLD VINCENT stands at a cul-de-sac at the end of a long, straight deserted street. He places a basketball in the middle of the street to represent the SUN and begins to unwind the huge reel of string attached to the ball. 11-YEAR-OLD ANTON walks a pace behind him. Several yards along the trail a bead is threaded through the string to represent the planet MERCURY.

ANTON
How many astronauts are there, anyway?
Vincent ignores him and continues to reel out the string.

ANTON
I bet I could be one.
Vincent stops and regards his younger brother with contempt.

VINCENT
You're standing on Venus.
Anton lifts his foot. There is a bead beneath it.

INT/EXT. CAR / SATELLITE DISH. DUSK.
VINCENT has developed into a handsome 17-YEAR-OLD. His spectacles hidden, he and a YOUNG WOMAN are necking in the front seat of a beat-up car, parked overlooking a huge satellite dish.
JEROME (VO)
I was popular enough until it got around that I wasn't a long-term proposition.
The love-making intensifies. The YOUNG WOMAN moves down
Vincent's chest and unzips his fly.
JEROME (VO)
Those who didn't know already could easily find out for themselves. It was certainly no problem coaxing the information out of me.
We remain on Vincent's face as he climaxes. The YOUNG WOMAN turns her head away from the spent Jerome and, out of his view, trickles semen from her mouth into a clear specimen vial.
JEROME (VO)
I didn't blame them. You need to know if a prospective husband can qualify for a mortgage or life insurance or can hold down a decent job.

INT. HOME. DAY.
In the living room of their modest home, the dark-haired, 17- year-old, bespectacled VINCENT sits opposite his PARENTS. The crestfallen Vincent has a book on his lap entitled "CAREERS IN

SPACE".
MOTHER
(trying to break it gently)
Vincent, you have to be realistic. A heart condition like yours--

VINCENT
--I don't care. I'll take the risk.

MOTHER

It's not just you they have to be concerned about. Perhaps we could get you one of those new pacemakers. They're not perfect but--

FATHER
(letting his frustration show)
For God's sake, Vincent, don't you understand.
The only way you'll see the inside of a space ship is if you're cleaning it!
Vincent looks at his father in disbelief.
On a dinner table on the other side of the living room, 15-YEAR-OLD ANTON looks up from the biological specimen he is studying with a magnifying glass.

INT. PERSONNEL OFFICE - WAITING ROOM. DAY.
17-YEAR-OLD VINCENT hides his glasses in his pocket as he enters a WAITING ROOM. He gazes around at other APPLICANTS.
JEROME (VO)
My father was right. It didn't matter how much I lied on my resumé, my real C.V. was in my cells. Why should anybody invest all that money to train me, when there are a thousand other applicants with a far cleaner profile? Of course, it's illegal to discriminate -
"genoism" it's called - but no one takes the laws seriously.
As Jerome enters the office, we focus on the doorhandle he has just touched.
JEROME (VO)
If you refuse to disclose, they can always take a sample from a doorhandle...
Vincent hesitates before shaking the PERSONNEL OFFICER's outstretched hand.
JEROME (VO)
...or a handshake...
We focus on Jerome's envelope attached to his application form sitting on the Manager's desk.
JEROME (VO)
...even the saliva off your application form.
Sitting opposite the manager, Jerome's face falls. The manager puts a clear, plastic cup in front of Jerome.
JEROME (VO)
But for the most part we know who we are.
And if all else fails, a legal drug test can just as easily become an illegal peek at your future in the company.
Vincent saves the Manager the trouble and exits the office, leaving the cup where it sits.

EXT. BEACH. DAY.
17-YEAR-OLD JEROME walks up the beach to find 15-YEAR-OLD ANTON sitting with the YOUNG WOMAN Vincent had previously dated.
JEROME (VO)
I didn't blame Anton for his free ride. You can't blame someone for winning the lottery.
The Young Woman hastily departs.

LATER the two brothers face each other on the sand. Anton is the more statuesque of the two.

ANTON
(cocky)
You sure you want to do this?
Vincent's answer is to walk towards the water. Anton smiles mockingly at his brother's grim "game face" and follows.
From an aerial view we watch VINCENT and his younger brother, ANTON, swim beyond the breakers.
JEROME (VO)
It was the last time we swam together.
Out into the open sea, like always, knowing each stroke towards the horizon was one we had to make back to the shore. Like always, the unspoken contest.
We watch the two young men swimming stroke for stroke. They swim far out, beyond the point. Suddenly ANTON starts to slow, his strokes becoming labored until he becomes motionless in the water. He begins to sink like a stone. VINCENT, realizing Anton is no longer beside him, turns back to lend support.
Vincent takes him in a lifeguard hold and begins to nurse him back to shore. Finally the two boys are coughed up onto the shallows. They collapse, just beyond the waterline, exhausted, gasping for air. ANTONIO and MARIA arrive on the scene. ANTON is the first to recover while VINCENT clutches his side, his face screwed up in pain. Maria kneels down and starts to administer to Vincent but his father, Antonio, is unable to conceal his anger and contempt for Vincent.

ANTONIO
Vincent, you damn fool! You could have killed
Anton with your ridiculous contest! Why should he risk his life to save yours?! When are you going to get it through your thick head--you can't compete with your brother! Why try?!
Maria takes Antonio aside. Anton and Vincent exchange a look.

ANTON
Why didn't you say anything?

VINCENT
Why didn't you?
(staring back at his father knowingly)
It's okay. It's the way they want it.
JEROME (VO)
It confirmed everything in the minds of my parents - that they had taken the right course with my younger brother and the wrong course with me. It would have been so much easier for everyone if I had slipped away that day. I decided to grant them that wish.

INT. HOME. NIGHT.
ANTON stands at the mantlepiece in the dimly-lit living room.

He gazes at a framed family portrait - Vincent's face has been torn out of it. He suddenly spies VINCENT exiting the front gate, carrying a suitcase. Anton goes to shout Vincent's name but the words don't get out.

EXT. GATTACA. DAWN.
A pick-up truck, packed with a CLEANING CREW, pulls into the rear of the building. They are no longer strictly the migrant workers we have come to expect but rather a mixture of ethnicities - all members of a genetic underclass that does not discriminate by race.
As VINCENT exits the truck and turns towards the camera, we discover that he has now matured into the man we have come to know as JEROME. The only visible differences are the glasses he wears and his hair, still naturally dark.
JEROME (VO)
Like many others in my situation, I moved around a lot in the next few years, getting work where I could. I must have cleaned half the toilets in the state.
We follow VINCENT through the course of a day. Cleaning restrooms, toilets, picking up litter, sweeping, washing windows - gazing at the AEROSPACE WORKERS below. The building is part of the Gattaca facility, located near a shuttle launch site. Throughout the day, with the regularity of 747's, Vincent spies rocket ships in the distance, launching into the sky.
Jerome's is the only head that turns and looks up. Long after the sun has set, Vincent is still working. Another rocket ship lights up the darkness. Vincent gazes forlornly into the heavens.

EXT. GATTACA - GLASS WALL. DAY.
VINCENT cleans a window from the outside, staring in at the arrogant GATTACA EMPLOYEES entering the security channels - a smaple taken from their fingertips. Jerome, in a trance, constantly cleans the same spot of glass. He fails to notice an Older Janitor, CAESAR, appear beside him.

CAESAR
When you clean the glass, Vincent, don't clean it too well.

VINCENT
(confused)
What do you mean?

CAESAR
(glancing to the Gattaca workers)
You might get ideas.

VINCENT
But if the glass is clean, it'll be easier for you to see me when I'm on the other side of it.
Caesar smiles at Vincent's cockiness.

INT. GATTACA. DAY.

VINCENT empties garbage into a dumpster adjacent to Gattaca.

His attention is drawn to something in the trash. A discarded manual on Celestial Mechanics and Navigation. He wipes food residue off the corner.

INT. ASTRONOMY & TELESCOPE SHOP. DAY.
A forest of telescopes on tripods in an astronomy shop. VINCENT enters the store with a bucket and squeegee and immediately goes to clean the storefront window. The STORE OWNER looks up from his tabloid - "STAR" magazine.

OWNER
Where's Earl?

JEROME
He fell. Lucky it was only the second floor.
The owner nods and returns to his magazine. When he looks up again one of his tripods is missing its telescope and Jerome is nowhere to be seen.

INT. IN-VALID HOUSING PROJECT. NIGHT.
JEROME returns to his bare apartment. He removes the cloth covering the bucket to reveal a dumpy-shaped telescope snugly wedged inside. He starts to pour over his collection of textbooks. Other tattered space paraphenalia adorns the wall.
JEROME (VO)
Of course the best test score in the world wasn't going to get me in the front door unless I had the blood test to go with it.

EXT. GATTACA. NIGHT.
While his fellow WORKERS sit on the steps at the service entrance to Gattaca, passing around an unlabeled bottle of clear liquor, VINCENT sits some distance away studying his text book.
In the absence of a computer, he practices typing commands on a keyboard handdrawn on the flap of a cardboard box.
A tiny, seedy-looking man, GERMAN, forties, appears from nowhere and takes a seat beside him.

GERMAN
(offering his hand)
Vincent, I'm German--
(anticipating Vincent's response)
That's my name.
He looks the apprehensive Vincent up and down.

VINCENT
What do you think?

GERMAN
(shrugs)

I think I could do something
(glancing to the text book) provided you know what you're doing and you can meet the terms.
Vincent pulls a plastic e-money card from his overalls.

GERMAN
You got a photo of yourself?
Vincent produces a snapshot of himself - torn from the family portrait. German feeds the snapshot into the pocket-sized computer he carries. The picture is instantly scanned and appears on the computer's small color screen. German returns the photograph and hastily departs.
CAESAR, the elderly janitor, notices German's exit.

CAESAR
(to Vincent)
I thought I told you not to get any ideas.
High up the side of a building, washing windows, VINCENT pauses occasionally to practice typing commands on his cardboard keys - viewing a screen in his imagination - or the nightsky itself.
He hears his name being called.

GERMAN
Vincent...Vincent...

VINCENT
(staring through his glasses)
German, is that you?

GERMAN
Vincent, come down. I've found him.

INT. IN-VALID HOUSING PROJECT. NIGHT.
GERMAN leads VINCENT through a maze of corridors.
JEROME (VO)
For the genetically superior, success is easier to attain but is by no means guaranteed. After all, there is no gene for fate. And when, for one reason or another, a member of the elite falls on hard times, their genetic identity becomes a valued commodity for the unscrupulous.
One man's loss is another man's gain.
He gives a conspiratorial nod to another passing DNA BROKER, both men carrying their palm-top computers.

GERMAN
(enthusiastically reading from data on his portable screen as he walks)
He has the heart of an ox. He could run through a Goddamn wall--if he could still run. Actually, he was a big college swimming star.

VINCENT
I hope he's not just a body.

GERMAN
No problem. Before he dropped out he was an honor student, the right majors--

VINCENT
How do I square the accident?

GERMAN
(still reading data from his palm-top computer)
It happened in Australasia. He checked in yesterday. No family complications, no record he ever broke his neck. As far as anybody's concerned, he's still a walking, talking, fully-productive member of society.
You just have to get him off the pipe and fill in the last two years of his life.
(correcting himself)
Excuse me, your life.
German has stopped walking as if they have arrived.

VINCENT
(looking around for a likely candidate but finding none)
Where is he?
German reaches towards a PARAPLEGIC sitting in his wheelchair in the stairwell directly in front of them, his head slumped, an incriminating bong nestled in his lap. German pulls the man's head up by the hair. EUGENE. Depsite the patchy, unkempt beard and thick glaze over his eyes he bears a striking similarity to Vincent. Vincent holds a mirror beside the face of the lethargic Eugene to compare his own reflection.

GERMAN
(smiling confidently
What did I tell you? Which one's the mirror?

VINCENT
(still not fully convinced)
That's the hair color in his profile?
German checks an entry in his computer: "HAIR: BLONDE"

GERMAN
Yeah.

VINCENT
(touching his own dark strands)
I'd have to bleach my hair.

GERMAN

(irritated, impatient)
Why are you inventing problems? You two are a couple of goddam clones. You look
so right together, I want to double my fee.

VINCENT
(a thought occurs, addressing the paraplegic for the first time)
How tall are you?

EUGENE
(deadpan)
Four foot six.
Vincent grins, realizing that Eugene is referring to his seated height. There is an instant
connection between the two men.

VINCENT
Okay, how tall did you used to be?

EUGENE
(apathetic, still under the influence of whatever he's been smoking)
Six one.

VINCENT
(to German, disappointed)
He's too tall.

GERMAN
(shrugs)
You can wear lifts.

VINCENT
Even with lifts I'm never that tall.

GERMAN
There's a way.

INT. BACKSTREET SURGERY. NIGHT.
In a primitive operating theatre, VINCENT lies on a table, his lower legs masked off
for surgery. The SURGEON switches on a surgical saw and lines it up with handdrawn
incision marks.
Metal struts are ready to elongate his legs.

INT. IN-VALID HOUSING PROJECT - APARTMENT. DAY.
GERMAN wheels the dazed EUGENE into the apartment, cluttered with space
paraphenalia. One wheel of his rusting wheelchair is flimsily held on with wire.
VINCENT follows behind on crutches, both lower legs in casts and cross-braces.
Vincent signs the contract German puts in front of him.

EXT. STREET OUTSIDE A BAR. DAY.
EUGENE, glassy-eyed, strides out of a bar, past camera and into the street. We hear a squeal of brakes and a sickening thud.

INT. HOUSING PROJECT - APARTMENT. DAY.
EUGENE awakens with a scream, bathed in sweat, arms bound to a bed - the only real piece of furniture in the room. VINCENT, sitting on a crate beside him, soaking a towel in a bowl of water, is taken by surprise. Eugene continues to scream and thrash, fighting against his bindings. Vincent stuffs the towel into Eugene's mouth and holds onto his arms.
JEROME (VO)
I confess, at first I wondered if I had rescued a man who was already dead.

INT. HOUSING PROJECT - APARTMENT - BATHROOM. NIGHT.
VINCENT holds EUGENE's head over the toilet bowl as he vomits violently. Eugene's paralysis and Vincent's broken legs make the operation doubly difficult.
Finally Eugene has nothing left in his stomach to vomit. He drops to the floor in exhaustion. Vincent, also exhausted from the effort of holding Eugene over the bowl, joins him on the broken linoleum. Both men stare up at the ceiling that carries a map of the constellation.

VINCENT
You okay, Jerome?

EUGENE
(ironically referring to their mutual immobility)
Yeah. You want to go dancing tonight?
Vincent smiles.

INT. HOUSING PROJECT - APARTMENT. NIGHT.
EUGENE turns his nose up at the plate of boiled meat and potatoes that VINCENT puts in front of him. Vincent catches the look.

VINCENT
What's wrong with it?

EUGENE
I think I'd better choose the menu. After all, you're learning how to be me, I'm not learning how to be you.

VINCENT
(shrugs)
Suit yourself.

EUGENE

(trying to be more diplomatic)
Listen, I don't want you to think I'm ungrateful
--I know you and that little broker--what do you call him?

VINCENT
German.

EUGENE
You're both going to a lot of trouble--
(trying to be tactful)
Maybe you can con somebody into believing you're me to get your foot in the door--but
once you're inside, you're on your own. I'm sure you're sincere...
(glancing to the space paraphenalia)
...but I was being groomed for something like this myself. Even without the accident I
don't think I would have made it. My point is--how the hell do you expect to pull this
off?
Jerome merely stares back as if the thought of failure has never occurred to him.

VINCENT
(shrugs and states it simply)
I don't know exactly, Jerome.

EUGENE
(laughing)
At least you're honest.
(a thought occurs)
Call me by my middle name--Eugene--If you're going to be Jerome, you may as well
start getting used to it.

**NB: FOR THE REMAINDER OF THE SCREENPLAY "VINCENT" IS REFERRED
TO AS "JEROME".**
INT. HOUSING PROJECT - APARTMENT. NIGHT.
JEROME looks through Eugene's personal effects, including a photograph album. He
is drawn to a swimming medal inside the album at a page displaying a photo of a
wealthy, austere
MOTHER - Eugene evidently comes from money.
Even as he wheels into the room in his rickety wheelchair we see that EUGENE has the
bearing of someone of good breeding. He has a bag of blood on his lap. More blood is
being drawn from his arm through an IV. Eugene catches Jerome looking at the album.

JEROME
(guiltily closing the book)
I have to know where you come from.

EUGENE

If anybody asks, tell them the truth-- your family disowns you. You are a disappointment, Jerome.

JEROME
(referring to Eugene's medal, impressed)
What about this?

EUGENE
Wrong color. It's silver.
(tossing the bag of blood to Jerome)
It's not easy living up to this.
Eugene wheels away.

INT. HOUSING PROJECT - APARTMENT. DAY.
JEROME practises writing with his right hand, trying to replicate Eugene's signature.

EUGENE
(wheeling by, looking over Jerome's shoulder at the signature)
It needs work.

JEROME
(rueful)
You had to be a right-hander.

EUGENE
Noone orders southpaws anymore.

INT. HOUSING PROJECT - APARTMENT. DAY.
A pair of spectacles lie on the bed. JEROME, still wearing his twin casts, sits behind an optometrist's portable examining device. GERMAN hovering in the background, an OPTOMETRIST custom-fits JEROME with gossamer thin contact lenses.
JEROME (VO)
Myopia is a dead giveaway - one of the earliest and most justifiable of the quality-of-life corrections. Anybody with impaired vision is certain to be suffering from all the other deficiencies of a "nonadvantaged" birth.

GERMAN
(inspecting the lens in Jerome's eye)
It's no good. I can see an edge. He may as well walk in there with a cane.

INT. HOUSING PROJECT - APARTMENT. DAY.
The Optometrist has been replaced in the living room with a
BLACK MARKET DENTIST who bonds JEROME's small, gapped teeth to match EUGENE's perfectly straight, white picket fences.

INT. HOUSING PROJECT - APARTMENT. DAY.

Hair already bleached and cut to match Eugene's hairstyle,
JEROME sits in a chair against a hastily erected white paper backdrop. From his wheelchair, EUGENE puts the finishing touches to Jerome's hair. He wheels himself out of the way.
The final accomplice in Jerome's deception, a BLACK MARKET
COMPUTER GRAPHICS DESIGNER, takes Jerome's photo with a video camera. Manipulating the captured image, the Designer morphs
Jerome's face into the face of Eugene. The resulting photo that spits out of a printer is neither one nor the other but an acceptable combination of the two.

INT. HOUSING PROJECT - APARTMENT. DAY.
EUGENE is starting to prepare Jerome's specimen bags for the first time. He winces in pain as he plucks several hairs from his head. JEROME, now out of his casts, prepares job applications.

EUGENE
(still grimacing, referring to the follicles)
You really need that much?

JEROME
More than that. You'll get used to it.

EUGENE
(yanking out another hair)
God, what wouldn't you do to leave the planet?

JEROME
(inspecting a hair follicle)
Leave? Just a few million years ago every atom in this hair--in our bodies--was a part of a star.
I don't see it as leaving. I see it as going home.

EUGENE
(marvelling at Jerome's earnestness)
God, you're serious, aren't you?
Jerome ignores him. Having learnt his lesson, he hands the envelopes to EUGENE to lick the flaps.

INT. HOUSING PROJECT - APARTMENT. DAY.
JEROME is doing a late-minute cram on a geriatric computer from the late 1990's. Checking the time, Jerome hurriedly picks up the shirt that EUGENE has been ironing from a prone position on the floor.

JEROME
It's not too late to back out.

EUGENE
You don't know what a relief it is not to be me. Are you sure you want the job?
Jerome contemplates the question for a moment.

JEROME
What about you? What's in this for you, Eugene?

EUGENE
(referring to the bladder bag he wears)
Listen, I bag this stuff anyway. It may as well pay my rent.
Jerome hurrise to the bathroom where, with some difficulty, he inserts his urine device
for the first time. The new improved
Jerome emerges into the living room ready for his interview.

INT. GATTACA CORPORATION - TESTING LAB. DAY.
JEROME emerges from a bathroom and hands a TECHNICIAN his plastic cup full of
fraudulent urine and inserts it into the analyzer.

TECHNICIAN
(reading off the profile)
Congratulations.

JEROME
(perplexed)
What about the interview?

TECHNICIAN
(referring to the cup)
That was it.

EXT. GATTACA. DAY.
JEROME, scarcely able to disguise his delight, exits Gattaca, trying not to stare at the
superb specimens who are now his
"colleagues".
JEROME (VO)
The majority of people are now made-to-order.
What began as a means to rid society of inheritable diseases has become a way to design
your offspring--the line between health and enhancement blurred forever. Eyes can
always be brighter, a voice purer, a mind sharper, a body stronger, a life longer.
Everyone seeks to give their child the best chance but the most skilled geneticists are
only accessible to the priveleged few.
In a nearby park MODEL CHILDREN from MODEL PARENTS play together.
JEROME (VO)
Anyone who is the product of an altered
DNA is proudly referred to as a "DAN",
"self-made man or woman", "man-child".

INT. HOUSING PROJECT - APARTMENT. NIGHT.

JEROME wheels EUGENE out of their housing project. He takes in the neighborhood for the last time. We focus on a POOR COUPLE cradling an INFANT.

JEROME (VO)

Those parents who, for moral or, more likely economic reasons, refrain from tampering with their offspring's genetic makeup or who fail to abort a deprived fetus condemn their children to a life of routine discrimination.

We glimpse other PEOPLE in the neighborhood. They appear poor but, for the most part, physically normal. However a pall of gloom hangs over them.

JEROME (VO)

Officially they are called "In-Valids"*. Also known as "godchildren", "men-of-god", "faith births",

"blackjack births", "deficients", "defectives",

"genojunk", "ge-gnomes", "the fucked-up people".

[* "IN-VALID" pronounced as in "an invalid license"]

JEROME (VO)

They are the "healthy ill". They don't actually have anything yet - they may never.

But since few of the pre-conditions can be cured or reversed, it is easier to treat them as if they were already sick.

As they enter a car, driven by GERMAN, Jerome spies a beautiful young GIRL, 11, sitting on the steps of the housing project, staring forlornly into space. While there is no outward sign of any deficiency, she is somehow aware that she is damaged goods.

Jerome glances in the rearview mirror.

JEROME (VO)

By means of a donor I have cheated the system for the last four years to open doors that would otherwise be closed to me.

Jerome wheels Eugene into the palatial condominium complex where the two men now reside.

INT. GATTACA. PRESENT DAY.

We return to JEROME's reflection in the glass. Other GATTACA EMPLOYEES are gradually gathering behind him.

JEROME (VO)

In the guise of Jerome Morror I have risen quickly through the ranks of Gattaca. Only one of the Mission Directors has ever come close to discovering my true identity.

We now see what Jerome has been gazing at through the window the whole time - the sight that has brought a hush to the complex. Through an open office door lies the body of a large man - the MURDERED DIRECTOR, lying where he has just been discovered, in a pool of his own blood.

JEROME (VO)

Strange to think, he may have more success exposing me in death than he did in life.

Jerome wipes his eye and also goes to investigate. We focus on an extreme close up of his EYELASH. Loosened by Jerome's hand, it breaks free and floats gently down to the floor where it comes to rest.

INT. GATTACA AEROSPACE CORPORATION. MORNING.
DETECTIVE HUGO, late-forties, wearing a crime-scene hygenic suit and gloves and a full clear mask - looking more like a surgeon or a toxic waste worker than a detective - places a blood- spattered computer keyboard alongside the Director's shattered skull. The indentations match the blunt corner of the keyboard.
Hugo detaches the dangling keyboard from its parent computer and seals the likely murder weapon in a marked, transparent plastic bag.
A CREW of similarly-suited homicide detectives systematically vacuum the surrounding office area with metallic, industrial- looking mini-vacs. Once each work space has been vacuumed, the transparent plastic vacuum bag is detached, sealed and labelled.
OTHER DETECTIVES video the scene with camcorders. Video prints spit out of the cameras for instant inspection.

EXT. GATTACA - LANDSCAPED GARDENS. DAY.
A silicon police tape cordons off the crime scene. From the landscaped garden, a crowd of GATTACA EMPLOYEES view the proceedings through the glass walls.

EMPLOYEE 1
(staring at the Director's body)
Awful.

EMPLOYEE 2
Yeah, awful it didn't happen sooner.
Nervous smirks from nearby employees. We focus on JEROME.
Standing slightly apart from the others, he does not appear to share the joke, or perhaps even hear it. Jerome watches, wide- eyed, as a DETECTIVE approaches his work station with a mini- vac. A chill goes through Jerome as the detective's cleaner passes over his desk.
Jerome is distracted by a smear on the window, obstructing his view. Without thinking, he breathes on the glass and rubs the smear away with his elbow. Nearby, elderly janitor, CAESAR notices Jerome's fastidious act and reads the panic in Jerome's eyes.
DIRECTOR JOSEF suddenly appears at Jerome's shoulder.
Standing a pace behind the Director, computer notepad in hand, is IRENE.

DIRECTOR JOSEF
You're lucky to be getting out of this.

JEROME
We're still going ahead as planned?

DIRECTOR JOSEF
The launch window is only open until week's end. Tragic though this event may be, it hasn't stopped the planets turning.
He glances towards a group of Detectives headed by HUGO.

DIRECTOR JOSEF
You'll have to excuse me, Jerome. I have to meet with the authorities--naturally, we're co-operating in any way, although I won't tolerate a major disruption.
(as he departs)
I wish I was going with you, Jerome.
As the pair depart, Jerome and Irene exchange a glance. Irene is also aware of Jerome's unease.

INT. GATTACA - CORRIDOR. DAY.
We focus on JEROME's eyelash, still lying on the floor.
A huge crescent-shaped hair that fills the screen. Suddenly there is a roar of a mini-vac and the eyelash is sucked up. We follow the eyelash's journey, down the throat of the cleaner into the specimen bag where it is sucked against the bag's clear, plastic wall.

INT. GATTACA - COMPUTER COMPLEX. DAY.
The DIRECTOR's corpse is sealed in a plastic bodybag and wheeled away on a gurney. The blood and other body matter from the murder scene is sucked up by a portable wet-vac and the sample bag appropriately labeled.

EXT. GATTACA - COURTYARD CAFETERIA. DAY
A chime sounds over the P.A. follwed by an announcement.

ANNOUNCER (OC)
Thank you for your co-operation. Please return to your work stations immediately.
The PROGRAMMERS get to their feet en masse and begin filing into the work room.

EMPLOYEE 3
(sarcastic aside)
What, no counselling?

INT. GATTACA COMPUTER COMPLEX - DIRECTOR'S OFFICE. DAY.
A WOMAN ASSISTANT whose keyboard was used in the attack has to pause as a MAINTENANCE WORKER gives her work station a final spray to return it to its former pristine condition. A new keyboard is plugged into her monitor to replace the one taken as evidence.

INT. GATTACA COMPUTER COMPLEX. DAY.
JEROME opens his desk drawer to check his comb, now plucked completely clean. He carefully places two of Eugene's hairs to the comb and scatters another bag of fraudulent matter around his work station.

INT. GATTACA - SIMULATOR ROOM. DAY.
In a large, bare room a simulator does a slow dance back and forth on its hydralic legs, miming the path of the space craft Jerome will soon be aboard. The simulation ends and JEROME exits the simulator through a small door. IRENE hesitantly approaches, carrying a slim electronic tablet.

IRENE
Excuse me, Jerome. I'm sorry to bother you.
Jerome turns, not displeased by the interruption.

JEROME
No bother.

IRENE
(referring to her notepad)
I've been asked to compile a log for the investigators--they want to know everyone's
whereabouts last night.

JEROME
Last night? I was at home.
Irene makes a note with her stylus.

IRENE
Can that be, er, verified? Were you alone?

JEROME
No it can't be verified. Yes I was alone.
Irene makes another note.

JEROME
(wry smile)
Looks bad, doesn't it, Irene? What about you? Where were you last night?

IRENE
I was at home.

JEROME
Were you alone?

IRENE
(hesitant)
Yes.

JEROME
(teasing)
So we don't know for sure about you, either.

IRENE
(wary, wondering where the conversation is headed)
No.

JEROME
Why don't we say we were together?

IRENE
(confused)
Why would we do that?

JEROME
I have better things to do this week than answer the foolish questions of some flatfoot.
Don't you?
Irene contemplates the question.

JEROME
(gently pressing)
Well, shall we say we spent the evening together?
Irene is still unsure whether or not Jerome is serious.

IRENE
To be convincing, Jerome, I would have to know what that was like.
Irene turns and departs. Jerome watches her go.

INT. EUGENE'S CONDOMINIUM. NIGHT.
The paraplegic EUGENE, seated by the window, meticulously cuts a long fingernail
into numerous clippings. He places the clippings in small plastic bags and seals them.
He then begins to fill tiny sachets with blood. He turns as he hears JEROME enter down
the spiral staircase with the groceries.

EUGENE
You didn't forget the truffles?
JEROME places the items in the refrigerator in the bathroom and retrieves a bottle of
vodka - the vodka incongruous-looking beside the blood and urine specimens. Joining
Eugene at his workbench, he pours them both a drink.

EUGENE
(sensing something amiss, trying to keep his humor)
Who died?

JEROME
The Mission Director.

EUGENE
(misinterpreting the deadpan remark)
You wish.

JEROME

They found him in his office this morning-- beaten so bad they had to check his nametag.
Eugene takes in the news, a smile broadening across his face.

EUGENE
What an act of benevolence--a service to the community. So that's it. Now there's nothing between you and ignition.

JEROME
He was still warm when they confirmed.

EUGENE
(confused by Jerome's attitude)
This calls for a celebration. Doesn't it?

JEROME
The place is crawling with Hoovers.

EUGENE
So what? You didn't kill him, did you?
Jerome shoots him a glance for the inappropriate remark.

JEROME
That's not the point.

EUGENE
(scoffing)
Hey, how much of you can be there? Even if the
"J. Edgars" do find something, in a week--
(glancing up to the night sky) you'll be slightly out of their jurisdiction.
(gently chiding)
Come on, we've got to get drunk immediately.

JEROME
(still tempering Eugene's enthusiasm)
You're going to have to earn your supper. I've got my final physical tomorrow.
Jerome wheels Eugene's chair to a specially constructed platform that allows the wheels to spin in mid-air. Jerome tapes an electrode to Eugene's chest and attaches the wire to a slim recording device. Eugene begins to spin the wheel of the chair faster and faster. Jerome monitors Eugene's steady heartbeat through a set of headphones.

INT. GATTACA AEROSPACE CORPORATION - COMPUTER COMPLEX. NIGHT.
The complex is virtually empty - only a handful of the hundreds of PROGRAMMERS working late into the night. IRENE approaches

JEROME's work station on the pretext of delivering some documents. Trying to act casually, she looks under the papers on his desk, then opens the top desk drawer.

We see an EXTREME CLOSE UP of the comb lying there - the two hairs trapped between the teeth of the comb. Irene removes one of the follicles and drops it into an envelope she is carrying.

INT. 24-HOUR SEQUENCING LAB. NIGHT.

"SEQUENCING-WHILE-U-WAIT". Similar to a 1-hour photo lab, the store - little more than a booth - displays a price list on the wall. "FULL SEQUENCE - $80". IRENE waits in line with a cross- section of other CUSTOMERS. She checks the contents of the envelope that contains the hair.

The YOUNG WOMAN in line ahead of her allows the TECHNICIAN to take a swab from her full lips with a Q-tip.

TECHNICIAN
How old?

YOUNG WOMAN
(confused)
Me?

TECHNICIAN
(mustering patience, referring to the Q-tip)
The specimen.

YOUUNG WOMAN
(proudly)
I kissed him five minutes ago. A real good one.
Overhearing, several PEOPLE in the line snicker.

TECHNICIAN
(long-suffering)
I'll see what I can do.
The technician hands the swab to an ASSISTANT. The Young Woman is handed a number and takes a seat. Irene hands her envelope over the counter. She too is handed a number. We follow
Jerome's follicle as another TECHNICIAN places it in an analyzing machine.

INT/EXT. SEQUENCING LAB / PARKING LOT. NIGHT.

The TECHNICIAN returns the envelope to IRENE along with a miniature compact disc.

TECHNICIAN
(remarking on the profile result)
9.4...very nice.
Irene does not appear to share the technician's enthusiasm.

She emerges from the sequencing lab and enters her car. Taking a palm-top computer from her purse, she inserts the disc into the computer. Jerome's counterfeit genetic profile appears on the screen. The details confirm her worst fears.

EXT. MICHAEL'S DINNER CLUB. NIGHT.
JEROME and EUGENE, dressed to the nines, pull up in the car to a darkened doorway in a poorly lit street. A VALET appears out of the shadows. Familiar with the car, he goes immediately to the trunk to retrieve Eugene's collapsible wheelchair.
Jerome tips the valet - a credit card wiped through a device.

INT. MICHAEL'S DINNER CLUB. NIGHT.
The chic, elegant establishment inside belies its darkened exterior. JEROME wheels EUGENE into a decadent dinner club full of an odd assortment of people. They are immediately greeted respectfully by MICHAEL, the owner and maitre d'.
Jerome and Eugene are obviously regulars.

MICHAEL
Good evening, gentlemen. Your table is ready.
(referring to Jerome's mission)
Not long now, sir. You'll be upstairs before you know it. We're going to miss you.

JEROME
Not as much as I'll miss your Stroganoff.
I'd like to take one of your chefs with me.

INT. MICHAEL'S DINNER CLUB. NIGHT.
In a secluded booth JEROME and EUGENE toast from a bottle of
1999 vintage Bordeaux. Eugene drinks longer than Jerome.
Jerome dabs his mouth with a napkin. He fails to notice a minute FLAKE OF SKIN dislodged from his chin. We follow the flake as it comes to rest beneath the table.
LATER, Eugene and Jerome watch COUPLES dancing a samba on the dance floor. A WAITER vacuums the table with a discreet, handheld miniature vacuum while a WAITRESS clears the plates.
She accidentally drops a knife onto Eugene's leg.

WAITRESS
(aghast at the sight of his lifeless legs)
I'm so sorry. Did I hurt you?

EUGENE
(smiling, a trace of bitterness)
Honey, if you'd hurt me, I'd be cured.
Eugene, the worse for drink, gropes for the waitress's leg but she easily avoids his clumsy pass.

EUGENE

You want to meet a real-life spaceman?
Jerome, always aware, scanning the club, suddenly spies
NAPOLEON, his Gattaca colleague, on the other side of the room. Napoleon is taking
a hit from a vial concealed in his hand. Jerome abruptly turns his back to avoid being
recognized.

JEROME
Let's get out of here.

EUGENE
(knocking back his drink, misinterpreting the hasty departure)
You're right, there's more atmosphere where you're going.

INT/EXT. CAR. NIGHT.
Driving along the freeway, Jerome's car suddenly dives down an escape road. EUGENE
looks sideways at JEROME.

JEROME
You drive.

INT/EXT. CAR. NIGHT.
The car careens around and around a small circular building - a cloud of dust billowing
up behind the car. We focus on a
BRICK wedged against the car's gas pedal.
EUGENE is at the wheel, JEROME in the passenger seat.
The hard turn is repeated with increasing recklessness, Eugene fighting to control the
bucking car.

EUGENE
(screaming in both fear and exhilaration)
I gotta stop!! I gotta stop!!

JEROME
Keep going!! Keep going!!
Finally the car spins to a halt in a cloud of dust. When the dust settles it is revealed that
they have been circling the base of a huge satellite dish in a desolate location.

EXT. SATELLITE DISH. NIGHT.
EUGENE lies on the hood of the car, leaning against the windshield, drinking from a
bottle of vodka. In the background, the unmanned satellite dish. JEROME relieves
himself against the building at the base of the satellite.

EUGENE
(gently chiding Jerome over the joyride)
You idiot. You could ruin everything with a stunt like that.
Eugene spies a spacecraft launching from Gattaca city.

EUGENE
(gazing up into the night sky)
At least up there your piss will be worth something.
(smiling at the thought)
You'll all be showering in it, right?

JEROME
(zipping his fly)
And drinking it. It's like Evian by the time it's filtered.

EUGENE
(referring to the rocket ship)
What is that one?
Jerome doesn't bother to look in the direction of the craft but merely glances to his watch. He joins Eugene on the hood of the car.

JEROME
(looking at his watch)
11.15 to the port. A maintenance crew.

EUGENE
How long do you stay up there before you go?

JEROME
A day or so.

EUGENE
(beaming)
I still can't believe they're sending you to the Belt--you of all people--never meant to be born, on a mission to discover the origin of life.
Eugene laughs to himself and passes the bottle to Jerome.

JEROME
You should be going instead of me.
Jerome taps Eugene's lifeless legs with his foot.

JEROME
Up there they wouldn't be a problem.

EUGENE
(glancing heavenwards, shaking his head)
You know I'm scared of heights.

INT. CRIME LABORATORY - AUTOPSY ROOM. NIGHT.

The body and clothing of the MISSION DIRECTOR, lying on a metal examining table is scanned with a blue-light magnifying instrument. Fingernail specimens are taken for analysis. In another area of the laboratory, the labelled vacuum bags are attached to analyzers and the contents sucked out and automatically identified. ID names and photographs of GATTACA
EMPLOYEES begin appearing on a computer screen at high speed along with other personal details - all data automatically logged for later review.
The photographs and personal details of JEROME and IRENE flash past, amongst the faces of other employees.
We focus on a magnified close up of JEROME'S EYELASH, still clinging stubbornly to the side of its specimen bag. We continue to follow its journey as it is finally sucked into the analyzer.

INT. CRIME LAB - ANALYZER MACHINE. NIGHT.
Inside the machine, a minute, cell-thin sliver is sliced from
JEROME'S EYELASH and analyzed.

INT. INVESTIGATOR'S CRIME LAB. NIGHT.
A severed HUMAN TONGUE sits on a tray in a sterile, sealed chamber. Using gloves that protrude through the chamber's glass wall, face buried in a binocular eyepiece, the INVESTIGATOR takes a swab from the tongue.

INVESTIGATOR
(to the tongue, as he inserts the tip of the swab into an analyzer)
Let's see what you've got to say for yourself.
A FEMALE ASSISTANT, looking on, hardly has time to smile at the remark before information begins to appear on a nearby computer terminal. The computer gradually builds a portrait of the owner of the tongue using genetic predictors. The Investigator wanders over to the window as his Assistant reads the information from the screen.

ASSISTANT
The tongue is male. Mature. Blonse hair.
Brown eyes. Light complexion. Between
5'11 and 6'1. Pronounced Caucasian nose.
Thin lips. Weak chin. Lobeless ears.
Prematurely balding. Slightly bow-legged.
Broad shoulders. Barrel chest...
(pause)
Blind.

INVESTIGATOR
(interest piqued)
Blind?
(mildly amused, checking the monitor for himself)
The tongue is blind?

ASSISTANT
(confused)
Who cuts out the tongue of a blind man?

INVESTIGATOR
(shrugs)
Someone who is mindful that the blind still speak.
The INVESTIGATOR is alerted by the chime of his nearby computer.
On the screen, he discovers the face of 20-YEAR-OLD VINCENT and the accompanying flashing message: TRACKING IN-VALID
883000181105-10 - NEW DATA -

INT. CONDOMINIUM COMPLEX - PARKING GARAGE. NIGHT.
Having plugged his car into an overnight charger, JEROME pushes
EUGENE in his wheelchair to the elevator. Bottle in hand,
Eugene leans over and vomits on the ground. Jerome shakes his head resignedly.
Eugene looks drunkenly up at Jerome.

EUGENE
(sarcastically referring to the pool of vomit)
I'm sorry. Did you want it?
Jerome meets Eugene's gaze. There is a trace of bitterness in Eugene's drunken smile.

EUGENE
Let me get it for you.
Eugene bends down to scoop up some vomit with his hand but the elevator arrives and Jerome quickly wheels him away. Eugene's head flops to the side as he passes out.

INT. EUGENE'S CONDOMINIUM. NIGHT.
JEROME unlocks EUGENE's condo and wheels his chair inside. We see their reflection in a full-length mirror as Jerome pushes
Eugene to the bedroom. After removing Eugene's soiled clothing, he heaves the tall man from the chair and onto the bed.

EUGENE
(maudlin, sobbing like a child)
I'm sorry. I'm sorry.

JEROME
(attempting to comfort)
It's okay, Eugene.

EUGENE
You know I wasn't drunk--I knew what I was doing when I walked in front of that car--

JEROME
--What car?--Go to sleep.

EUGENE
--I walked right in front of it. I was never more sober in my life.
Jerome looks at Eugene's lifeless legs, trying to cover his shock at the revelation.

JEROME
It's all right.

EUGENE
(grabbing Jerome by the collar)
I'm proud of you, Vincent.
Eugene's head falls back onto the pillow.

JEROME
(smiling to himself)
You must be drunk to call me Vincent.
But Eugene does not reply, drifting into sleep once again.
Jerome pulls a blanket over him.
On the verge of leaving, Jerome's attention is drawn to a wall on the far side of the room. Approaching the wall, near
Eugene's mirrored closet, he detects a faint mechanical whir coming from inside the adjacent condominium. Jerome contemplates investigating but exits the condominium instead
- climbing the spiral staircase to his own condominium.

INT. JEROME'S CONDO - LIVING ROOM. NIGHT.
JEROME fastidiously vacuums with an upright cleaner. Using a hose attachment he cleans around a picture frame that contains
Jerome's original computer keyboard handdrawn on the flap of a cardboard box.

INT. GATTACA - COMPUTER COMPLEX. DAY.
In the vast room of COMPUTER PROGRAMMERS we pull-focus to discover that we have been filming the complex through the transparent specimen bag containing JEROME'S EYELASH.
On the mezzanine floor overlooking the scene of the crime, the INVESTIGATOR holds the bag, transfixed by the lash. The lead homicide detective, DETECTIVE HUGO, finishes interviewing a GATTACA SECURITY GUARD and approaches the Investigator.
A large telescope in the background.
Although Hugo is deferential to his more youthful superior, his body language betrays his displeasure. Hugo clearly does not relish the Investigator's involvement in his case.

DETECTIVE HUGO

I don't understand why you were dragged out here, Sir. It's hardly worth wasting your time--a no-nothing case like this.

INVESTIGATOR
(gently rebuking his subordinate)
A man's dead, Detective.

DETECTIVE HUGO
Of course, Sir. We're checking the entry log, alibis, grudges...

INVESTIGATOR
Grudges?

DETECTIVE HUGO
(looking out over the balcony)
I look around, I see a lot of dry eyes.
The Director was not...
(searching for the words)
...universally loved. He was leading the cut-backs in the program. You're looking at a room full of motives.

INVESTIGATOR
(shaking his head adamantly, referring to the bag in his hand)
No, this is your man.

DETECTIVE HUGO
(not so convinced)
With respect, Sir--it may be the only unaccountable specimen but the profile suggests--

INVESTIGATOR
--What about his profile?
Hugo refers to a print-out of 20-YEAR-OLD VINCENT's profile including his Genetic Quotient. (The fifteen-year-old photo of
Vincent now bears little resemblance to his assumed identity.)

DETECTIVE HUGO
According to this, he's a sick man. Congenital heart condition. Who knows how long the specimen has been here but there's an 80 percent chance the owner of that eyelash has already died himself from natural causes.

INVESTIGATOR
(terse)
So there's a 20 percent chance he's not dead.
Detective Hugo goes to comment further, then revises his remark in his head before speaking.

DETECTIVE HUGO
Even if this Vincent Luca is alive, is it likely he could bludgeon a man to death?

INVESTIGATOR
No. Not likely.
The Investigator's tone suggests that the identity of the culprit is no longer a matter for debate. There is an awkward pause before the Detective falls into step with his superior.

DETECTIVE HUGO
I take it you're thinking along the lines of a robbery gone sour--a thief disturbed in the act?
The Investigator merely shrugs.

DETECTIVE HUGO
(skeptical)
Of course that doesn't jibe with what we found. This was an angry killing.

INVESTIGATOR
(glancing to the profile in Hugo's hand)
Who knows with these "deficients"? His profile indicates a proclivity for violence.

DETECTIVE HUGO
(trying to appear co-operative)
I'll run a crossover on the eyelash for any family or associate connections--

INVESTIGATOR
--I've already run it. There's no record of any living relative.

DETECTIVE HUGO
What a pity.

INVESTIGATOR
(irritated, glancing to the sample bag)
Detective Hugo, it's a simple case of lost and found. All we have to do is locate the man who's minus an eyelash and this murder will solve itself.
We focus on JEROME at his work station. Although he continues to work, he clrarly feels the presence of the INVESTIGATORS on the mezzanine floor behind him.
A MEDICAL DIRECTOR approaches the programmer in the neighboring work station - NAPOLEON, the programmer Jerome encountered in the nightclub the previous evening.

MEDICAL DIRECTOR
Napoleon, you're late for your substance test.
Napoleon looks up, ashen-faced. Jerome intervenes.

JEROME
Director, Napoleon's helping me today.
The Director regards both men suspiciously.

MEDICAL DIRECTOR
Well, you take it for him, Jerome.
The Medical Director departs. Napoleon, stunned by the reprieve, approaches Jerome's
work station and pretends to study the program on his computer screen.

NAPOLEON
Why did you do that?

JEROME
(exiting to the testing lab)
Don't worry about it.

INT. GATTACA - TESTING LAB. DAY.
From behind we observe JEROME standing in front of LAMAR, issuing forth his
steady stream of fraudulent urine.

**EXT. GATTACA AEROSPACE CORPORATION - WORKOUT CENTER.
DAY.**
Twenty GATTACA EMPLOYEES, identically-outfitted men and women, run in a
perfectly straight line towards the tranquil lake of the picturesque grounds, never getting
any closer to their goal.
They run at a steady 10mph on twenty identical state-of-the-art treadmill machines
sunken into the floor and arranged in a uniform row facing a floor to ceiling window.
The strain is beginning to show on many of the faces. The heartrate of each employee
is monitored via a wireless electrode attached to the chest.
Outside in the sunshine the next batch of twenty EMPLOYEES limbers up in readiness
for their physical. JEROME's only preparation consists of thoughtfully dragging on a
cigarette while staring out at the man-made lake. His nonchalant attitude disheartens
nearby colleagues, including
IRENE who is amongst a group of workers excused from the run by benevolent, over-
protective TRAINERS.

TRAINER
You're excused, Irene. You may resume your duties.
On the way into the work-out facility Jerome stubs out his cigarette in a stainless steel
ashtray. Only we are aware of the slim credit card-sized recording device that he
furtively slips out of his cigarette pack and secrets in his hand. As he takes his place on
one of the treadmills and adheres the cordless electrode to his chest, Jerome
surreptitiously attaches his device to the underside of the running machine's control
panel.

INT. GATTACA - WORK-OUT OBSERVATION ROOM. DAY.

From a mezzanine floor above the work-out room, LAMAR, the medical officer, monitors computer read-outs displaying the pace and pulse of the runners on each treadmill machine.

INT. GATTACA - WORK-OUT CENTER. DAY.
One by one the GATTACA EMPLOYEES drop out until JEROME is the sole remaining runner. Several of the other employees stand around and watch Jerome run as they towel off.
He appears under little duress, staring directly ahead, seemingly in a trance. As we focus on his chest, only we are aware of the sound of his furiously pounding heart making a lie of his calm exterior.

INT. GATTACA - WORK-OUT OBSERVATION ROOM. DAY.
Jerome's heart registers a far more measured beat on the computer in the observation room. The DIRECTOR is at LAMAR's shoulder, beaming proudly.

LAMAR
(marveling at Jerome's heartrate)
Six miles later it's still beating like a
Goddamn metronome. I could play piano by that heartbeat of his.
The INVESTIGATOR and DETECTIVE HUGO enter the observation room, escorted by IRENE.

DETECTIVE HUGO
Director Josef, this is our lead Investigator.
The two men exchange a polite handshake. However the
Investigator is immediately taken with the SOLE RUNNER with his back to him, on the treadmill below.

INVESTIGATOR
How often do you test, Director?

DIRECTOR JOSEF
Often.

INVESTIGATOR
(intrigued)
Surely you know what you have.

DIRECTOR JOSEF
We have to be certain. Once they're up, we can hardly turn the boat around.
On the treadmill below, Jerome glances to his watch as he runs, the distress starting to show. Caught up in the conversation,
Lamar has forgotten to end the work-out. Remembering, he finally presses the "WARM-DOWN" button, slowing the treadmill.

LAMAR
(still marveling at Jerome)
I swear if I went to lunch and came back, he'd still be there.
We focus on Jerome's recording device attached to the bottom of the control panel. It clicks to a stop, indicating that the bogus heartbeat recording has ended before the workout.
The heartbeat monitor in the observation room suddenly races from 80 to 250 beats per minute. Lamar catches the discrepancy out of the corner of his eye but before he can take a second look, Jerome has whipped his electrode from his chest. The physician shrugs it off as a glitch in the machine.
The Investigator has turned his back on Jerome to face the
Director.

INVESTIGATOR
We believe we have a suspect.

DIRECTOR JOSEF
What a relief.

INVESTIGATOR
(referring to the profile of VINCENT on Hugo's computer notepad)
This unaccountable specimen was found in the south wing corridor.
In the room below, Jerome nonchalantly steps off the treadmill, stealthily retrieves the recording device from beneath the control panel and returns it to his cigarette pack.
He casually wipes off drops of sweat from the machine with a towel, briefly glances to Irene with the Investigators and exits to the locker room.
The Director idly regards the image of VINCENT on Hugo's handheld screen. He does not recognize the face.

DETECTIVE HUGO
An age enhancement is being prepared as we speak.

DIRECTOR JOSEF
(referring to his assistant)
Irene will make it available to security.

INT. GATTACA - LOCKER ROOM. DAY.
JEROME wears his assured smile all the way along the corridor and into the now empty locker room. He exchanges a cheery greeting with an exiting COLLEAGUE, enters a shower stall, closes the door behind him and promptly collapses on the shower stall floor.
The effects of the gruelling work-out are only now apparent. No longer sucking up the pain, he gulps air into his oxygen-starved lungs, his heart looking for a way through his tightened chest.
He writhes in agony on the white-tiled floor - a brutal reminder of the physical frailty he seeks to disguise.

EXT. GATTACA - GARDEN. LUNCHTIME.
In Gattaca's perfectly landscaped gardens JEROME, dressed and recovered from his ordeal, joins his COLLEAGUES for lunch at one of the umbrella-covered tables. While most of the others pick at unappetizing salads and take their individualized medication, Jerome carries a steak sandwich on his tray.
The sight of the juicy steak is greeted with envious looks from his colleagues. Jerome pretends not to notice and rubs it in by liberally sprinkling salt onto the meat.
However when Jerome looks over towards IRENE, she avoids eye contact. When she abruptly gets up and leaves, Jerome follows - thinking twice before depositing the napkin in the nearby trashcan. A janitor reaches for the napkin. It is the Old Janitor, CAESAR, from Jerome's former life.

CAESAR
I'll take care of that for you, Mr Morrow.
The two men exchange a conspiratorial smile.

EXT. GATTACA - WIND FARM. AFTERNOON.
A forest of wind turbines, supplying energy to the aerospace complex. However the blades of the turbines are motionless in the still afternoon. JEROME finally catches up with IRENE. She turns, unsurprised by his appearance. Standing beside her, he looks out over the complex as if he too has come for the view.

JEROME
(eyes fixed on the view)
We were looking at each other. You stopped.
Irene, also keeps her gaze ahead.

IRENE
I'm sorry. I didn't mean anything.

JEROME
(shrugging as if it makes no difference to him)
We were just looking.

IRENE
I know about you.
Jerome turns to her, startled, trying to read her face. Irene takes a deep breath and abruptly plucks a long, dark hair from her head.

IRENE
(offering the hair to Jerome)
Here, take it.
Jerome, confused, takes the hair - more in reflex than intent.

IRENE

(a challenge)
If you're still interested, let me know.
Jerome contemplates the hair in his fingers for a moment, then deliberately lets it fall to the grounf.

JEROME
(never taking his eyes from her)
Sorry, the wind caught it.
Irene meets his gaze. There is not a breath of wind. The hair lies, plainly visible on the ground.

EXT. GATTACA AEROSPACE COMPLEX. AFTERNOON.
As JEROME and IRENE walk between the wind turbines, Jerome pretends not to notice that Irene keeps furtively checking the pulse on her wrist. They pause in the shade.

JEROME
(as if making conversation)
Have they found our friend?

IRENE
Friend?

JEROME
(shrugs)
It was a mercy-killing after all.

IRENE
They found an eyelash.

JEROME
Where?

IRENE
In the South Wing.

JEROME
Does it have a name?

IRENE
Just some In-Valid. Vincent--
(trying to come up with the last name)
--somebody.
Jerome turns away to disguise his alarm. He quickly recovers.

JEROME
Perhaps we ought to celebrate, Irene.

IRENE
(a smile playing around her lips)
You celebrate, Jerome?

INT. EUGENE'S CONDO. NIGHT.
EUGENE talks irritably on the phone, examining a container from a newly opened case of hair bleach.

EUGENE
(into phone)
--I know what I ordered. I ordered "Honey
Dawn" and you sent me "Summer Wheat".
JEROME descends the staircase, taking the steps two at a time.
He immediately goes to the refrigerator, removing trays of samples. Eugene abruptly hangs up the phone.

JEROME (OC)
Call German.

EUGENE
Any particular reason?

JEROME
(collecting up sample bags from the work bench)
We can't stay here.

EUGENE
What are you talking about?

JEROME
They think I offed the Director.
Eugene wheels himself over to Jerome, unconcerned.

EUGENE
What makes them think that?

JEROME
They found my eyelash.

EUGENE
(a flicker of anxiety)
Where?

JEROME
In a corridor.

EUGENE
(blas once again)
Could be worse. They could have found it in your eye.
Jerome half-smiles despite the situation.

JEROME
(resuming his collection of samples)
Come on--we're taking off.

EUGENE
I'm not going anywhere. Less than a week to go.
Not on your life--

JEROME
--You don't understand, they'll make the connection, they'll hoover again. We should
cut our losses.

EUGENE
(angrily grabbing a tray from Jerome's hands)
Where is your head, Jerome? You're acting like a guilty man. They won't marry the
eyelash to you. They won't believe that one of their elite navigators could have suckered
them for the last five years.

JEROME
They'll recognize me.

EUGENE
(scoffing)
How could they recognize you?
(referring to the torn photo of
20-year-old Vincent on the wall)
I don't recognize you. Anyway, you don't have a choice. You run, you may as well sign
a confession, turn us both in right now. No, we stick this out-- find out what we can but
change nothing. This is a minor inconvenience is all it is. We've taken worse heat than
this.
(angry now)
Jesus, if I'd known you were going to go belly up on me at the last fucking gasp, I
wouldn't have bothered. You can't quit on me now. I've put too much into this.
(returning the samples to the fridge)
Besides, this stuff is mine. I had other offers, you know. I could have rented myself out
to somebody with a spine. You want me to wheel in there and finish the job myself?
(meeting Jerome's gaze)
We'll take off all right, from pad 18 just like we planned.
Jerome slumps down in a chair, Eugene's tirade starting to get to him.

EUGENE
And keep your lashes on your lids where they belong. How could you be so careless?

JEROME
I'm sorry.
(reluctant admission)
I think I was crying.
Eugene is uncomfortable at the notion.

EUGENE
Well save those tears.
Jerome shrugs awkwardly and pours them both a drink.

JEROME
You really had other offers?

EUGENE
(shrugs)
I'm sure I could have.

INT. CONDOMINIUM - INCINERATOR. NIGHT.
The naked JEROME scrapes away at his skin with even greater ferocity than usual.
After exiting the incinerator, he deposits all the incriminating trash he has collected
during the day into the furnace and ignites the gas.

INT. EUGENE'S CONDOMINIUM. NIGHT.
From outside, a car horn sounds. JEROME, in a formal suit and spectacles, abruptly
enters the condominium. He goes to a closet and starts searching through Eugene's
clothes.

JEROME
Mind if I borrow a tie?
EUGENE is more interested in the car parked outside the condominium. IRENE sits in
a convertible Citroen DS, dressed in a classic but provocative black suit. Unaware that
she is being observed she touches up her lipstick in the rearview mirror.

EUGENE
So it's not just the Hoovers who've got you rattled.

JEROME
You're the one who said not to change anything.
She's my ear to the investigation.

EUGENE
(skeptical)
Is that all?

JEROME
I've got enough on my mind without that.

EUGENE
If you say so.
(referring to the ties in Jerome's hand)
The stripe.

JEROME
(agreeing with the selection)
Good choice.
Jerome fumbles with the knot. From his chair, Eugene knots
Jerome's tie for him. Jerome is intrigued that for once Eugene is abstaining - he has not
touched his drink.

JEROME
Not thirsty?
(referring to the fridge)
We've got enough virgin samples to last us the week.

EUGENE
I don't feel too good. I think I'm still drunk from last night.

JEROME
Never stopped you before.
(regarding Eugene's head)
And for God's sake stop plucking your hair.
Someone went to a lot of trouble to make sure you wouldn't go bald.

EUGENE
If I were you I'd worry about myself.
(nodding to Jerome's spectacles)
Haven't you forgotten something?
Jerome pockets the spectacles and enters the bathroom for his contact lenses. The horn
sounds outside the window a second time and Jerome hastily exits. We stay with
Eugene. Irene catches a glimpse of him before he moves away from the window.
Jerome emerges from the building.
As the couple drive away, Eugene wheels himself to the full length mirror. He regards
his own reflection for a moment and opens the mirror - a disguised door opening into
the adjacent apartment. A cloud of condensed water vapor billows out.
GERMAN, the DNA Broker, emerges with an ENGINEER.
He sends the engineer on his way and joins Eugene at his desk.
Eugene hands German a credit card that he wipes through his computer.

GERMAN

We still need to overhaul the back-up generator.
(fixing Eugene with a penetrating stare)
What's going on, Eugene, I thought he was going away, not you--you going on vacation?

EUGENE
(looking away)
You got it, German.

GERMAN
(nodding thoughtfully)
You deserve it.

INT. CONCERT HALL - AUDITORIUM. NIGHT.
JEROME and IRENE step over feet, apologizing as they go, eventually finding their seats in a box in a sold-out concert hall.
On the stage below, a YOUNG PIANIST - a teenage prodigy - has already taken his place at the keys of a grand piano. The pianist removes his white gloves and begins to play - an extremely complex and beautiful piece we have never heard before. IRENE looks to JEROME. He is clearly caught up in the music.

EXT. IN-VALID HOUSING PROJECT. NIGHT.
The music from the piano recital continues under the following contrasting action. A huge, brooding housing project. PEOPLE hang around on street corners. Menace in the air - a feeling of impending violence.
Suddenly unmarked police cars appear from all directions, blocking any escape route. Dozens of PLAINCLOTHES DETECTIVES pour out of the cars and onto the street.
People scatter, many running straight into the arms of the
Detectives. OTHERS, spilling out of the housing project, are also immediately apprehended.
The Detectives quickly weed out those suspects not fitting
Jerome's description - WOMEN, OLD MEN and TEENAGERS. They are shepherded off the street. A line of IN-VALIDS is formed several hundred yards long. Detectives begin to laboriously move along the line, taking finger-prick blood samples from each suspect - instantly confirming their identities with portable analyzers worn on their hips. As if having the idea at the same time, TWO SEPARATE MEN suddenly bolt from the line, knowing that their blood will incriminate them. Other Detectives, watching for such escape attempts, esaily apprehend them and escort them to a waiting police van. With the raid under control, DETECTIVE HUGO indicates to the
INVESTIGATOR that it is safe to exit his car. The Investigator appears irritated, only half-glancing at the TWO MEN already in custody, apparently certain that neither one is his suspect.

DETECTIVE HUGO
(enthusiastic)
Not our fish, but sometihng stuck in the net.
The Investigator clearly does not share Hugo's enthusiasm. The

Detective offers the Investigator an age enhanced photograph, computer-generated from the last existing photo of VINCENT as a 20-year-old.

DETECTIVE HUGO
This is the age enhancement we're working with.
The Investigator ignores the photo, preferring instead to trust his own eye as he wanders along the line of suspects.

DETECTIVE HUGO
(referring to the line-up)
As you requested, we've kept the parameters wider than usual.
The MEN they scrutinize are hardly mutants - the differences between an IN-VALID and a DAN are subtle at best. Some shorter, some wearing glasses, some with receding hairlines or bald, many with no discernable physical difference at all. The Investigator is only halfway down the line before he turns and starts walking back to his car.
The mystified Detective Hugo follows his superior.

INVESTIGATOR
We're in the wrong place. We're wasting time.

DETECTIVE HUGO
This is the most likely location--
The Investigator wheels on Hugo, suddenly angry, clearly unused to having his judgement questioned.

INVESTIGATOR
--There's that word again. I have a feeling
This man doesn't play the odds, Detective. Not exactly a slave to probability. Is it "likely" that a man who has successfully eluded authorities for fifteen years--a brutal killer--is going to come to us now like a lamb?

DETECTIVE HUGO
(taken aback by the outburst)
Is there something more we should know about this suspect, Sir? I mean besides what's on his sheet.

INVESTIGATOR
Since going underground, traces of this In-Valid have shown up at the scene of four serious felonies. Do you need any more than that?

DETECTIVE HUGO
With respect, Sir, many perfectly innocent citizens have left specimens at as many crime scenes. Maybe he's just unlucky.

INVESTIGATOR

I don't like anybody this unlucky.
(pause)
Widen the sweep. The West side. Draw a five mile radius around Gattaca. Hoover some of the classier establishments. Random car stops.

DETECTIVE HUGO
We're already getting complaints about frivolous search.

INVESTIGATOR
This is a murder investigation. The public should be happy to co-operate, to get this disease off the streets.

INT. CONCERT HALL. NIGHT.
A standing ovation. The YOUNG PIANIST on the stage bows deeply, soaking up the applause of the AUDIENCE. The pianist tosses one of his white gloves into the front row where it is caught by an adoring FAN. The second glove he tosses up to the box where
JEROME and IRENE are standing. Jerome snares the glove out of the air and immediately hands it to Irene. She promptly slips the glove on her own hand.
The glove fits snugly over her five fingers. However one finger of the glove remains unfilled. Jerome is stunned to realize that it is a six-fingered glove.

IRENE
(catching his look of astonishment)
You didn't know?

JEROME
(trying hard to convince)
Yes...yes...

IRENE
(picking up a resentment, confused)
You're angry--

JEROME
Why would I be angry? It was beautiful.
He quickly turns away to lead the applause. On stage, the pianist raises his hands to acknowledge the crowd. Both his hands contain a perfectly formed extra finger.

INT. IN-VALID HOUSING PROJECT - PROSTITUTE'S BOUDOIR. NIGHT.
From an upstairs window we observe the INVESTIGATOR's car cruise slowly back into the squalid housing project. A MAN is buckling his pants at the window.

JOHN
Shit! One of those Hoovers is back.
A prostitute, VALERIE, a slender, sylphlike beauty, joins him at the window.

VALERIE
It's alright. He's here to see me.
Her client looks at her askance. Despite her assurances, he hurries into his clothes anyway.

VALERIE
(to an unseen woman in the next room)
Sonja, I can't see anyone else tonight.

INT. IN-VALID HOUSING PROJECT - PROSTITUTE'S BOUDOIR. NIGHT.
The INVESTIGATOR, sits up in the bed, glass in his hand.
VALERIE lies on the tangled sheets, naked, making no effort to cover herself. She regards the Investigator curiously.

VALERIE
I don't understand you, Investigator.
The Investigator glances idly in her direction.

VALERIE
(teasing good-naturedly)
You hunt us by day and fuck us by night. Do you only get it up for In-valids?
The Investigator smiles and rejoins her on the bed.

VALERIE
Wouldn't you be happier with one of your made-to-order whores?

INVESTIGATOR
(gently stroking her hair)
You are so beautiful, are you sure you weren't altered? This is not the face, the body, of a Godchild. How could something so lovely be a product of chance?

VALERIE
Is that what keeps you coming back?
(meeting his gaze)
Look at you. Such angry, beautiful, perfect eyes.
Do you ever wonder what they would see if they weren't quite so perfect? They will never see what I see.
The Investigator tries to laugh off her assertion but his tight-lipped smile betrays his displeasure.

INVESTIGATOR
(a cruel edge to his voice)
You have so much wrong with you, you'll be lucky to see next year.
He roughly forces himself on top of her but she remains defiant.

VALERIE
Are you so much more alive, Investigator?

INVESTIGATOR
(parting her legs)
I'm not paying you to talk.

INT/EXT. IRENE'S CAR. NIGHT.
IRENE drives, JEROME at her side. Cars are being flagged down by uniformed POLICE OFFICERS. Irene slows down behind the car in front. Spying an OFFICER shine a flashlight in the eyes of the MALE DRIVER up ahead, Jerome wipes the contact lenses from his eyes and flicks them out of the passenger window when Irene is not looking.
An OFFICER approaches Jerome and, without a word, opens an electronic testing kit worn on his hip. He removes a sterilized
Q-tip and motions for Jerome to open his mouth so he can scrape a culture. Jerome waves his hand in front of his mouth, feigning embarrassment.

JEROME
(conspiratorial)
Better not.
(nodding in Irene's direction)
Don't want to give you a contaminated specimen...if you get my meaning.
IRENE plays along, shrugging coyly at the cop.
We see an EXTREME CLOSE UP of Jerome's hand as he furtively retrieves a hair follicle attached to his shirt cuff. With the hair already in his fingers, he pretends to pluck a hair from his head, faking a wince at the appropriate moment.
The cop, wearing transparent latex gloves, takes the follicle and places it in a receptacle in his kit. After a short moment the hair confirms JEROME's driving ID which appears on the kit's electronic screen. As the cop departs, Irene looks questioningly at Jerome.

JEROME
Thanks.
(answering her unasked question)
You never know where those swabs have been.
Irene nods, however clearly not convinced. She shakes the doubt from her mind.

IRENE
I want to show you something.
She accelerates away. We see the road ahead from Jerome's POV.
Without his contact lenses, it is a blur.

INT. MICHAEL'S CLUB. NIGHT.
After closing time, suited DETECTIVES vacuum the club in which

Jerome and Eugene dined the previous evening. MICHAEL, the owner, looks on disdainfully. Waiting in the background, the regular CLEANERS - most likely In-valids themselves - smirk to each other, enjoying watching the cops do their work for them.

EXT. OCEAN HIGHWAY. NIGHT.
With no place to turn the car around, IRENE parks on the cliff side of the six-lane highway. In the darkness she dashes from the car and, without a second thought, runs directly out into the heavy commuter traffic. Easily negotiating the on-coming cars, she emerges safely on the other side of the highway.
JEROME, rounding the car from the passenger side, is about to follow, when he suddenly pulls up sharply at the curb. We focus on his eyes, deprived of the benefit of their contact lenses.
From Jerome's POV, we see that the headlights rushing towards him are nothing but a series of fast-moving blurs - blurs that merge together. He is unable to distinguish between the vehicles or judge their distance.

IRENE
(calling back urgently from the other side, mindful of the light beginning to leak into the sky)
Come on! We'll miss it!
Irene stares expectantly back at Jerome with her 20/20 vision, unaware of his predicament. Jerome puts a foot off the curb at the wrong moment and is almost collected by an on-coming car.
Irene is taken-aback at his mistiming. Does she detect a squint on Jerome's face? To Jerome, the figure of Irene on the other side of the highway is merely a featureless shape but he feels her expectation. He touches the spectacles, still in his pocket, but they are an unthinkable option.
He shakes the idea from his head and turns back to the swiftly- flowing highway. He makes up his mind - he cannot allow himself to be shamed, even at the risk of life and limb. Hardly even glancing at the traffic, he suddenly bolts blindly across the road. Headlights hurtling towards him, cars fortuitously brushing past his heels, horns blaring. Jerome makes a final leap to the haven of the far curb, the rush of air from a large, fast-moving truck blowing him the final inches to the sidewalk.
Irene is stunned by the near miss. She is about to comment but
Jerome takes her by the arm and ushers her towards the dunes.

JEROME
Come on. We'll miss it.

EXT. BEACH. DAWN.
JEROME and IRENE huddle beneath an overcoat as the sun crests the horizon, staining the sky with an ochre blush.

IRENE
What did I tell you?

Jerome nods. However, to his eyes the rising yolk is nothing but an out-of-focus, abstract ink blot.

IRENE
I envy you, Jerome.

JEROME
You'll be next.

IRENE
I don't think so. The only trip I'll make in space is around the sun--
(letting a handful of sand slip through her fingers)
--on this satellite right here.
Irene turns to Jerome.

IRENE
(blurting out what's really on her mind)
--Listen, I don't want to waste your time and I really don't want you to waste mine.
I don't know what you're after but I have a feeling I'm not it.
Irene suddenly takes Jerome's hand and puts it up her sweater, onto her breast. Although taken aback, Jerome makes no effort to withdraw his hand.

IRENE
(enjoying his unease)
It's here. My heart.
(adding quickly)
I'm careful--weekly check-ups. I'm on a drug maintenance program, blood thinners, diet--
(slowly removing his hand)
I just want you to know what you'd be getting yourself into.

JEROME
What exactly is wrong?

IRENE
Nothing yet. I'll start experiencing symptoms in my late-fifties.
(matter-of-fact)
But unless they come up with something between now and then, I won't live much past 67.
Jerome's mouth drops a little, betraying his surprise at the statement from a woman plainly still in her twenties.

IRENE
Of course I think about it every day.

JEROME

(still not quite recovered from his surprise)
Of course.

INT. POOL. MORNING.
The INVESTIGATOR swims his race with the unseen opponent. The
Investigator's ASSISTANT, carrying a phone, tries to attract his attention.

EXT. JEROME'S POOL. MORNING.
JEROME sits at his own poolside in his robe, feet dangling over the edge, smoking a
cigarette. EUGENE, from his wheelchair, is applying bleach to Jerome's hair and
eyebrows with gloved hands.
At the same time, Jerome plays a sleight-of-hand game with a syringe.

EUGENE
How was your evening?

JEROME
Complicated. I couldn't stop her apologizing.

EUGENE
(teasing)
You are a catch. No doubt she's worried that she would lower the standard of your
offspring.
Everybody wants to "breed up".
(idly curious)
What's wrong with her?

JEROME
(trying to be blas)
You know how it is with these altered births
--somebody told her she's not going to live forever and she's been preparing to die ever
since.

EUGENE
You're not thinking of telling her, are you?

JEROME
Of course not. But she's have to know eventually.

EUGENE
(adamant)
She doesn't have to know. She doesn't want to know.
The camera travels down Jerome's scarred legs to find that the pool is completely
drained. We now realize that it never contained water.

A BARREN WASTELAND.

A desolate landscape, resembling the surface of the planet Mars.
We pull back to find that we are peering at this forbidding desert through a circular aperture.

INT. CRIME LAB. DAY.
The INVESTIGATOR lifts his head from the eyepiece of an electron microscope through which he has been examining a tiny fragment of skin - the skin is identified as belonging to 20-
YEAR-OLD VINCENT. DETECTIVE HUGO stands at the Investigator's side - his attitude more respectful in light of the discovery.
Detective Hugo points out a location on a computer-generated map.

DETECTIVE HUGO
(chagrined)
The skin flake was found in Michael's Restaurant.
The employees are all accounted for.

INVESTIGATOR
A customer? Does this Michael's cater to misfits?

DETECTIVE HUGO
(shifting the view of the map to include the Gattaca complex)
No. But one or two "borrowed ladders" have shown up there in the past.
The Investigator understands the significance. They wander over to a blow-up photograph of the 20-YEAR-OLD VINCENT.

DETECTIVE HUGO
We have to consider the possibility that he's playing somebody else's hand.
A smile gradually broadens across the Investigator's face.

INVESTIGATOR
(taking a perverse pleasure in the slowly dawning revelation)
Of course. He's a "de-gene-erate".
(glancing to a photo of the
Gattaca crime scene)
He works at Gattaca. Why else would we find the eyelash near the washroom? Nobody stops to take a leak during a murder.

DETECTIVE HUGO
(quickly covering himself)
It's still possible the eyelash specimen came from a janitor, delivery man--it could have blown in through an open window.
The Investigator appears not to be listening, his mind made up.

INVESTIGATOR
(mind racing)

He was afraid of being exposed. That's why he did it.

DETECTIVE HUGO
(puzzled)
It is hard to believe he could be one of their elite workers. You've seen their security system. They know who works there.
(referring to 20-year-old Vincent's profile)
Even if you ignore the man's expiration date, his profile suggests that he doesn't have the mathematical propensity let alone the stamina to pass their physicals.

INVESTIGATOR
Don't underestimate these imposters.

DETECTIVE HUGO
(skeptical, referring to a file of
Gattaca employee ID photos)
None of the ID photos match the enhancement.

INVESTIGATOR
(smiling to himself)
A man can change his face--but blood is forever.
Sample every employee within the parameters I gave you.
(pause)
Intravenous.
Hugo's mouth drops open at the mention of "intravenous".

DETECTIVE HUGO
(immediately protesting)
You know their workforce. Two-thirds at least fall into the category. We'll be closing down their operation for days.
(seeking a compromise)
At least go with a fingertip sample or urine.

INVESTIGATOR
(shaking his head)
Blood. From the vein.
The Investigator turns on his heel to prevent further protest.
The Detective and his ASSISTANTS exchange looks of exasperation behind the Investigator's back.

INT. GATTACA. DAY.
JEROME, drinking water, stands in front of a large video bulletin board. Among other things, it displays the electronic mugshot of 20-YEAR-OLD VINCENT alongside the recent computer generated age enhancement of his face.
Some distance away, CAESAR, the elderly janitor, discusses the mugshots with a YOUNGER JANITOR.

CAESAR
Look like anybody to you?

YOUNGER JANITOR
Not to me.

CAESAR
Ugly sonofabitch though, isn't he?
Jerome half-smiles, realizing that the conversation is for his benefit. Having made it clear that they do not intend to expose their former colleague, the two janitors continue their rounds.
Jerome crushes his paper cup. Forgetting himself, he drops the cup into the wastebasket.

INT. CRAFT. DAY.
JEROME familiarizes himself with the interior of a spacecraft under the supervision of DIRECTOR JOSEF and the MISSION
COMMANDER. The screen that Jerome sits at is identical to the one he operates in the computer complex - displaying asteroid
951 Gaspra.

DIRECTOR JOSEF
--Somewhere in the dust of Gaspra is the key.
(warming to his theme)
Back to the beginning of the book--the life we became. With the original building blocks who knows how far we can take "the godding".

MISSION COMMANDER
(wry smile)
Even someone as advanced as Jerome will be last year's model by the time we're done.

JEROME
(smiling back)
I wouldn't get your hopes up, Commander.
Irene enters the craft.

IRENE
Excuse me, Mr Morrow. The investigators have begun their testing.

DETECTIVE JOSEF
This is so inconvenient, Irene. They can make an exception for Jerome.

IRENE
I'm afraid not.

DIRECTOR JOSEF

I apologize, Jerome.

JEROME
It's not yor fault, Director.
(afterthought)
If your predecessor were still around we may not be going to Gaspra at all.
That's what I would call inconvenient.
Jerome exits the craft with Irene.

INT. GATTACA CORPORATION - CORRIDOR. DAY.
A line of MALE GATTACA EMPLOYEES snakes out the door and down the corridor. The INVESTIGATOR walks slowly down the line, trying to eyeball his suspect. Concentrating on the shorter, dark-haired men in the line, he looks straight past JEROME.
However, as the Investigator ignores him and walks by, we see a haunted look in Jerome's eyes.

INT. GATTACA - TESTING LAB. DAY.
Every available TECHNICIAN is working to accommodate the testing of the thousand or so PROGRAMMERS. Twelve testing stations operate simultaneously. A HOMICIDE DETECTIVE supervises each station. JEROME reaches the head of the line. He notes an exiting COLLEAGUE holding a cotton ball to his arm.
A NURSE directs Jerome to LAMAR's testing station. Lamar deposits the previous patient's labeled vial into a blood carousel under the watchful eye of a large DETECTIVE, clearly not relishing his assignment. Jerome rolls up his sleeve.

JEROME
(referring to the table lined with syringes)
What's with the plungers, Lamar? What are you doing, opening a blood bank?
The syringes are clearly not Lamar's idea.

LAMAR
(sarcastic)
The gentlemen of law enforcement are concerned that my testing methods may have been compromised.
Lamar inserts a fresh syringe into Jerome's arm. As Lamar draws the blood, Jerome suddenly flinches and flexes his arm violently, causing the needle to bend and buckle, exiting the skin from a second puncture point.

JEROME
Damn!!
Having pulled away from Lamar's grasp, Jerome withdraws the bent needle himself, blood still squirting from his vein.

LAMAR
(grabbing a nearby wad of gauze)

Jesus--I'm sorry, Jerome.
The large Homicide Detective winces and turns away from the red arcing spray, a splash
of blood spattering his shoes. In the midst of the commotion, with his practised sleight-
of-hand,
Jerome removes the vial from the syringe and replaces it with another concealed vial.

JEROME
(unfazed, putting Lamar at his ease)
You must be out of practise, Lamar.
Lamar hurriedly takes the syringe from Jerome.

LAMAR
(examining and removing the switched vial from the bent syringe)
I've got enough here.

JEROME
(regarding the squimish detective, as he holds the gauze to his arm)
Need any more, you can always get it off his shoes.
The Detective notices the spatter of blood across his brogues and, with a look of disdain,
wipes it clean. He tosses the incriminating tissue down a hygenically sealed garbage
shoot.
Lamar places Jerome's labelled vial in the carousel where it is immediately analyzed by
the computer. Jerome's "legitimate"
Employee ID code appears on the screen - "VALID". Another
EMPLOYEE enters the testing lab.

INT. GATTACA. DAY.
JEROME exits the testing lab with the gauze held to his arm.
IRENE is standing outside the door.

IRENE
So you didn't do it after all.

JEROME
(joking darkly)
I guess somebody beat me to it.

INT. GATTACA - MEZZANINE FLOOR. LATER IN THE DAY.
From above, the INVESTIGATOR and HUGO observe the final EMPLOYEE exit the
testing lab.
LAMAR, following the employee out of the lab, throws a look of vindication to the two
cops.

DETECTIVE HUGO
That's the last.

INVESTIGATOR
Something's not right.

DETECTIVE HUGO
(losing his patience)
He's not here. It's a blind alley.

INVESTIGATOR
(resolute)
No, we've missed something. We Hoover again.

DETECTIVE HUGO
We don't have the manpower.

INVESTIGATOR
Get it. From outside, if you have to.

DETECTIVE HUGO
From what budget?

INVESTIGATOR
(angered by Hugo's excuses)
I'll take it out of your damn pension if you question my authority one more time!
The INVESTIGATOR turns his back on his subordinate and idly contemplates the nearby telescope. Hugo resignedly relays the news to Director Josef who is standing some distance away.
Josef's immediate reaction is to march towards the Investigator,
Hugo trailing behind. DIRECTOR JOSEF collects himself as he notices the Investigator's hand on the telescope.

DIRECTOR JOSEF
Would you care to look--in the telescope?

INVESTIGATOR
Thank you, no.

DIRECTOR JOSEF
(still referring to the telescope)
One look through there and you would know why
I can't possibly allow you to disrupt operations any further.

INVESTIGATOR
(unfazed)
You're so unconcerned that you have a killer in your midst.

DIRECTOR JOSEF

Right now, your presence is creating more of a threat. I don't think you have any concept of what we do here--how meticulous our preparations must be. We are about to send twelve people through 140 million miles of blackness to rendezvous with an object the size of a house and the color of coal. So it's rather critical to point them in the right direction.

And we certainly don't need you looking over our shoulders. Besides, I don't believe there is any evidence that the killer is amongst us. I don't see too many other dead bodies littering the place.

INVESTIGATOR
(surveying the mostly empty facility)
No, but since there aren't too many live ones tonight either, you won't mind us conducting one further sweep. If he does not work here, then there should be no other trace of him.
(to Hugo)
I think you'd better get some people out of bed,
Detective.
(a thought occurs)
In the meantime we can re-check his favorite haunt.
Director Josef quietly seethes.

INVESTIGATOR
(to Josef, referring to the telescope)
You see, Director, I prefer my microscope.

INT. EUGENE'S CONDOMINIUM. DAY.
JEROME readies himself for an evening out - a bandage around his arm from the needle puncture. EUGENE wheels himself in.

EUGENE
Where are we going?

JEROME
(slightly guilty)
I'm sorry. I've got plans.

EUGENE
(feigning hurt)
Again?

JEROME
(referring to his bandage)
She's already got her doubts. I have to act like nothing's wrong.

EUGENE
I'm sure you'll be very convincing.

Jerome ignores the remark.

EUGENE
Where are you taking her?

JEROME
Michael's.
Eugene looks at him askance.

JEROME
Everybody goes there.

EUGENE
(incredulous, glancing around the room)
You may as well invite her here.

JEROME
(afterthought as he picks up his jacket)
Will you be okay?

EUGENE
Don't worry about your little pin cushion.
To be honest, I'm looking forward to having the place to myself.

JEROME
(seeing through the bravado)
We'll still be able to talk when I'm away.
The conversation will just keep getting longer.

EUGENE
How long?

JEROME
By the time I'm at the Belt, you phone and say, "How are you?" Forty-five minutes later
I reply, "Not bad. How are you?"

EUGENE
I guess I'd better have something important to say if it takes that long to get an answer.

INT. MICHAEL'S CLUB. NIGHT.
IRENE and JEROME step off the dance floor of the smoky, decadent dinner club and
take a seat at their table. Irene is agog at the strange assortment of PATRONS, the
cigars, the laden dessert trolleys. It is all slightly off from the pristine world she is
accustomed to.

IRENE

What is this place?

JEROME
(wry smile, enjoying her fascination)
You've never been here?
(a dessert trolley is wheeled up)
Let me order for you.
Jerome selects a chocolate torte from the trolley. Jerome savors a spoonful. Irene is tempted but then remembers herself.

IRENE
I'd better not.
She reaches for her elegant pill box. Jerome takes another spoonful.

JEROME
So sure of what you can't do. Do you even know what it tastes like, Irene?
Irene goes to deny it but cannot.
MICHAEL suddenly approaches the table with a WAITER in tow.
Irene is about to steal a taste of the dessert with her finger when their plates and glasses are whisked away and the table immediately hoovered. Michael whispers in Jerome's ear.

MICHAEL
Take the side door.
Jerome looks up in time to see DETECTIVE HUGO coming through the front entrance with several other DETECTIVES.

DETECTIVE
(to his colleagues)
Check for lenses, hairpieces--
A Detective shines a flashlight in the eyes of a MALE PATRON.
A SECOND DETECTIVE tugs the hair of a SECOND PATRON. Jerome takes Irene by the hand and escorts her out of the side exit.
Several other COUPLES make for the parking lot.

IRENE
Why are we leaving?

JEROME
(attempting to explain the hasty exit)
Those checks take forever.

EXT. MICHAEL'S CLUB - SIDE ALLEY. NIGHT.
Spilling out of the exit, JEROME and IRENE find a burly plain clothes DETECTIVE barring their way. Before the Detective can say a word, Jerome has wrapped his fist in

his jacket sleeve and smashed him in the face. He continues to beat the Detective until
he lies motionless on the ground.

IRENE
(stunned)
Jerome!
Spying other Detectives some distance away in the parking lot.
Jerome leads Irene out of a hidden side gate.

IRENE
What about the car?

JEROME
(grabbing her by the hand)
Let's walk.

IRENE
Who are they?

JEROME
(holding his bruised knuckles)
It's not safe. I shouldn't have brought you here.
Jerome drags Irene across a vast, desolate lot, lit only by moonlight. Feeling exposed,
he breaks into a run.

IRENE
I can't.

JEROME
(anxious)
Come on.

IRENE
My medication. I left it back there.

JEROME
We'll get it later.
(forcing her to look him in the eye)
Irene, please.
Irene realizes his seriousness. She begins to run with him.
The clearing is wider than Jerome anticipated. They are only halfway across - extremely
vulnerable if the Detective think yo look in their direction.

INT. MICHAEL'S. NIGHT.

The INVESTIGATOR is grilling MICHAEL, the club's owner. The investigator suspiciously regards the multitude of mini-vacs in the kitchen and the incinerator burning the refuse.

INVESTIGATOR
(an accusing tone)
You run a clean establishment.

MICHAEL
Are you a health inspector?

INVESTIGATOR
(showing Vincent's mugshot)
Do you recognize this man?

MICHAEL
My eyes aren't so good.

INVESTIGATOR
I bet.
Hugo calls out from the side door where he has discovered his fallen colleague.

HUGO
Sir.
The Investigator hurries to him.

INVESTIGATOR
(to the still dazed Detective, examining his injuries)
Did he hit you with his fist?

DETECTIVE
(head in his hands)
More like a hammer.

INVESTIGATOR
(reprimanding the beaten Detective)
Don't touch your face. Don't swallow.
Don't spit.
(to Hugo)
Quick, clean his teeth.
Hugo uses a flashlight and a small dental-like implement to try to pick skin from Jerome's knuckles from between the Detective's teeth. The Investigator finds the hidden side door.

EXT. DESOLATE LOT. NIGHT.

JEROME and IRENE continue to sprint across the enormous vacant lot in the moonlight, splashing through deposits of mud and water. Just as the gate opens in the distance, Jerome hurls
Irene into the safety of the undergrowth on the other side.
Irene, out of breath, desperately feels for her pulse.

IRENE
(upset, a strangled protest)
Are you trying to kill me? Are you?!
Don't you understand, I can't do that!
Jerome tenderly removes Irene's hand from her pulse.

JEROME
You just did.
Irene looks back across the vast clearing they have just negotiated, realizing what she has just done.
From across the other side of the clearing comes an echoing cry from the center FIGURE.

INVESTIGATOR (OC)
Vincent! Vincent!

EXT. MICHAEL'S. NIGHT.
The INVESTIGATOR is about to cry out Vincent's name once again when he realizes DETECTIVE HUGO and the other DETECTIVES are watching him, askance.

INVESTIGATOR
(to Hugo, covering his frustration)
What are you waiting for?

DETECTIVE HUGO
Where do we start?

INVESTIGATOR
We'll vacuum these streets if we have to.

DETECTIVE
(handing the Investigator Irene's pill box)
We caught them trying to flush these, Sir.
The Investigator carefully examines the heart pills.

EXT. IRENE'S APARTMENT. NIGHT.
JEROME walks IRENE to the steps of her apartment. Jerome thinks about departing but Irene takes him gently by the hand.

IRENE

So sure of what you can't do.
Jerome follows her inside.

INT. IRENE'S BEDROOM. NIGHT.
JEROME and IRENE climb a staircase to her bedroom. Without another word they begin to make love.
LATER THAT NIGHT, JEROME cannot sleep. He rises quietly so as not to disturb IRENE. He silently opens the double-windows of the upstairs bedroom. He carefully gathers his pillow from the bed and shakes it out of the window.
Slowly Jerome turns to gaze at the wood floor. In the moonlight we see an EXTREME CLOSE UP of a single hair lying on the floorboards. Jerome bends and picks up the hair, trying to identify it in the dim light. On his hands and knees he tries to clean the floor with a towel. Irene turns over in the bed. Jerome freezes but she continues to sleep. He realizes he may be spreading even more of his skin and hair over the floor.
Overcome with frustration and the enormity of his task, he begins to quietly weep.

EXT. A FIELD. DAWN.
A light shroud of mist hangs over the trees that encircle a grassy clearing beyond Irene's building. Something lies in the center of the clearing.
We jump-cut to an EXTREME CLOSE UP of two or three blades of grass. Bristles rain down on the blades. Withotu access to his incinerator, the crouched, naked figure of JEROME disposes of his whiskers, skin and hair in an open field. His clothes sit in a neat pile at his side. He pours glycolic acid over his body and scrubs at his back, feet and hands with a brush. There is a haunted, tortured look in his eyes as he tries desperately to rid himself of himself.

INT. POOL. MORNING.
The INVESTIGATOR swims obsessively in his aquatic treadmill.

INT. IRENE'S APARTMENT. LATER THAT MORNING.
Back in the bedroom, JEROME, partially dressed, holds IRENE in bed. She softly touches the scars on his shins.

IRENE
(referring to the shins)
What happened?

JEROME
You remember the '99 Chrysler LeBaron?
It's the exact height of the front fender.
(shrugs)
Looked right instead of left.

IRENE
(comforted by the thought)
So you're not so smart after all.

(awkward about raising the subject)
I want you to know--if it ever came to it--
I'd be willing to get an ovum from the Egg
Bank. In fact, I'd rather use a donor egg--
(quickly covering herself again)
--if it came to it.

JEROME
But "if it came to it" then it couldn't have your--
(searching for an appropriate body part)
--nose.
(stroking her face)
How perfect does your child have to be?

IRENE
(mildly irritated by what she perceives as his mocking)
You hypocrite. Do you think for one moment you'd be doing what you're doing if it
wasn't for who you are--what you are? Don't you get any satisfaction knowing that your
children will be able to live to a ripe old age unless they do something foolish?

JEROME
That's precisely what scaresme--that they won't do anything foolish or courageous or
anything--worth a Goddamn.
Irene is taken aback by Jerome's passion, regarding him in a new light.

INT. EUGENE'S CONDOMINIUM. MORNING.
EUGENE urinates into a large plastic container while drinking bottled water at the same
time. He already has several other containers of urine on the table beside him.

INT. GATTACA. MORNING.
The INVESTIGATOR and DETECTIVE HUGO keep a wary eye on the outfitted
DETECTIVES re-vacuuming the empty computer complex with their mini-vacs.

HUGO
(reading newspaper)
My wife and I--we're thinking of starting a family.

INVESTIGATOR
(shrugs, ambivalent)
Why not?

HUGO
These new personality corrections I've been reading about.

INVESTIGATOR
You worried about the cost?

HUGO
Not that.

INVESTIGATOR
(regarding Hugo with a condescending smile)
They said the same thing about myopia and obesity. You think your children would be less human if they were less violent, angry, spiteful? Maybe they'd be more human. From where I sit the world could stand a little improving.
We dwell on one DETECTIVE in particular, snatching a garbage bag from CAESAR, the janitor.

DETECTIVE
Don't touch that. It's evidence.
He puts a pile of discarded paper cups aside for later testing.

INT. GATTACA CORPORATION. LATER THAT MORNING.
In the vast, empty Gattaca complex the INVESTIGATOR inspects a specimen bag containing Jerome's paper cup with DIRECTOR JOSEF and DETECTIVE HUGO.

DETECTIVE HUGO
Positive saliva match. The cup was definitely used since the original sweep.

INVESTIGATOR
So we have two choices. Either our suspect came back to the murder scene for a drink of water and I don't know anybody that thirsty or...
(looking out over the empty complex)
...he is here.
(resolute)
We test again. You're right, Hugo, this was a desperate act. Someone had a lot to lose that night--perhaps their place in line.
(to Director Josef)
I'd like the profiles of everyone with an upcoming mission.

DIRECTOR JOSEF
(nervous)
Twelve have a mission within the week.

INVESTIGATOR
This time I will supervise each test personally.

INT/EXT. GATTACA. MORNING.
JEROME and IRENE walk towards the entrance to Gattaca. Spying the Homicide Investigation trucks parked at the rear of the building and the silhouette of the INVESTIGATOR in the doorway,
Jerome pulls up sharply. Irene notices his unease.

IRENE
What is it?

JEROME
I forgot something--something at home.
I'll see you later.
Jerome kisses her. Irene, also aware of the trucks, interrogates Jerome with her eyes.

IRENE
I'll miss you.
Jerome is still focussed on the entranceway.

IRENE
(looking skywards)
--when you go away.

JEROME
We could go together one day.
Irene considers the idea. She enters Gattaca alone.

INT. GATTACA AEROSPACE CORPORATION - COMPUTER COMPLEX. DAY.
IRENE prepares a stack of ID photos of CREW MEMBERS for the
INVESTIGATOR. She closely inspects the doctored photo of
JEROME, hesitating before adding it to the file.
The camera dwells on JEROME's vacant work station. The
INVESTIGATOR curiously regards the empty chair. He is accompanied by
DETECTIVE HUGO, DIRECTOR JOSEF and IRENE.

DETECTIVE HUGO
He's the only absentee.

DIRECTOR JOSEF
A little nausea. Quite common.

INVESTIGATOR
At least it's nothing contagious.

DIRECTOR JOSEF
(unduly agitated)
I will not permit any further testing on the eve of a mission. We're already counting
backwards.
The INVESTIGATOR ignores Josef and takes a pocket knife from his jacket. He prises
out the "ESC" key from Jerome's keyboard, places the key in a specimen bag and
deposits it in his jacket.

IRENE
(picking up a phone)
I'll call and let him know.
The Investigator gently but firmly removes the phone from
Irene's hand and replaces the receiver in the cradle.

INVESTIGATOR
Let's not spoil the surprise.
(to Irene)
I understand you can show us the way.
The anxious Director Josef calls out to protest one further time but the Investigator is
on his way out of the door.

EXT. STREET OUTSIDE GATTACA. DAY.
Outside the entrance to Gattaca, trying to hail a taxi, JEROME is startled to see a car
carrying the INVESTIGATOR, DETECTIVE
HUGO and IRENE roar out of the driveway. JEROME calls on his portable wristphone.

INT. EUGENE'S CONDOMINIUM. DAY.
EUGENE, at his window, filling sachets as usual, hesitates before answering the phone.

EUGENE
Hello?

JEROME (OC)
How would you like to be yourself for the day?

EUGENE
(nonchalant)
I was never very good at it, remember?

INT. EUGENE'S CONDOMINIUM / HALLWAY. DAY.
With a look of resolve, EUGENE hangs up the phone.
He wheels his chair up to the sweeping staircase and regards the first of many dozen
steps. The daunting staircase spirals away above him.

INT. INVESTIGATOR'S CAR. DAY.
HUGO drives. The INVESTIGATOR looks to IRENE in the rear seat.

INVESTIGATOR
(taunting)
You don't know who he is, do you, Irene?
He hands her the pill box found in Michael's.

INVESTIGATOR

You think you have problems?

INT. EUGENE'S CONDO/JEROME'S CONDO. DAY.
Having wheeled his chair out of sight, EUGENE eases himself out of his wheelchair and onto the floor. Using his elbows, commando-style, dragging his lifeless legs behind him, he proceeds to crawl across the floor and up the first step of the long spiral staircase. We observe his agonizingly slow progress up a staircase that, from Eugene's point of view, appears to have doubled in length.

EXT. CONDOMINIUM COMPLEX. DAY.
The INVESTIGATOR and DETECTIVE HUGO emerge from their car with
IRENE in tow. They take in the impressive complex - the
Investigator gets a glimpse of the empty pool. They approach the intercom at the entrance.

INT. JEROME'S CONDOMINIUM. DAY.
EUGENE, bathed in sweat, finally crests the landing of the staircase. No respite. As he drags himself across the floor the internal phone rings. He frantically stretches up and knocks the phone off its hook so he can talk from his prone position on the floor.

INT. CONDOMINIUM - LOBBY. DAY.
IRENE is on the phone, closely watched by the INVESTIGATOR and

DETECTIVE HUGO.
EUGENE (OC)
(through intercom, no trace of his distress)
Hello.

IRENE
(a moment's hesitation)
Jerome--?

EUGENE
Hello, sweatheart. Come on up.

INT. JEROME'S CONDOMINIUM. DAY.
With no mean effort, EUGENE finally manages to replace the phone on its cradle. He desperately crawls up onto the sofa.
However, spying the upright vacuum cleaner in the open closet, he is forced to crawl there and remove the vacuum bag. He frantically crawls back towards the sofa and stuffs the bag behind a cushion.

INT. JEROME'S CONDOMINIUM. DAY.
IRENE enters the door deliberately left ajar, closely followed by the INVESTIGATOR and DETECTIVE HUGO. EUGENE is propped up on the sofa, TV remote control placed in his useless hand to cover his paralysis. He has a stainless steel bowl next to

him and has crossed his lifeless legs for a more natural effect. Eugene calmy motions the confused Irene towards him.

EUGENE
Where's my kiss?
The Investigator scrutinizes Irene's reaction. With only the merest hesitation she takes her cue from Eugene and kisses him affectionately on the forehead. She perches herself on the arm of the sofa. Eugene takes the opportunity to rest his arm on her leg.

IRENE
Good to see you're feeling better.

EUGENE
Now you're here. Who are your "friends"?

IRENE
It's about the Director.

EUGENE
(feigning boredom)
Again?
The Investigator slowly circles Eugene, regarding him with the utmost scrutiny. He compares his face to the doctored Gattaca
ID photo - a passable likeness. Eugene bends towards the bowl and dry retches.

EUGENE
Forgive me for not getting up.
Irene puts a comforting hand on Eugene's shoulder.

IRENE
(to the Investigator)
Couldn't we do this another time?

INVESTIGATOR
I don't believe so.
Detective Hugo takes a seat in the chair beside the sofa and unpacks a syringe from the kit he carries.

DETECTIVE HUGO
This won't take a moment.
Detective Hugo swabs Eugene's inner arm. All eyes are trained on the tip of the needle as it punctures the vein.

EUGENE
(reassuring to Irene, referring to the blood flowing into the syringe)
It's okay. Maybe they can find out what I've got.

Under the Investigator's watchful eye, Detective Hugo withdraws the syringe and immediately inserts a small amount of the blood into the portable analyzer he wears. Naturally, it confirms that Eugene is Jerome.
Irene does her best to conceal her shock. Hiding his frustration, the Investigator distractedly tours the room while
Hugo packs up his gear. The Investigator idly toys with the telescope pointed out of the window.
Next he wanders towards the closet and reaches for the doorknob.

INVESTIGATOR
Mind if I take a leak?

EUGENE
As long as you don't do it in my closet.
(nodding to the other side of the room)
Over there.

INT. JEROME'S CONDOMINIUM - BATHROOM. DAY.
The INVESTIGATOR immediately pulls a specimen bag from his jacket pocket and closely inspects the stainless steel toilet and sink. They are both spotless. The shower stall is also scrupulously clean. He flushes the toilet and exits.
Lost in thought, the INVESTIGATOR approaches the closet again and wheels out Jerome's upright vacuum cleaner. He is disappointed a second time to find no vacuum bag inside. The
Investigator returns the vacuum cleaner to the closet and produces a mini-vac from Detective Hugo's crime bag.

INVESTIGATOR
(to Eugene, referring to ther mini-vac)
May I?

EUGENE
Clean the whole house if you want.

IRENE
(taking Eugene's lead)
Actually, the kitchen needs doing.
The Investigator switches on the mini-vac to take a specimen from the floor, then promptly kills the machine. Looking down, the Investigator notices the trail of Eugene's perspiration on the highly polished floor leading to the spiral staircase.
Eugene, reading the Investigator's mind, goes to call out but the words remain frozen on his tongue. Hugo follows his superior as they start to descend the stairs. Irene and Eugene are left staring at one another.

INT. CONDO - STAIRCASE. DAY.
JEROME catches the merest glimpse of the INVESTIGATOR and

DETECTIVE HUGO before he slips behind a doorway in Eugene's condominium.
Jerome anxiously regards Eugene's empty wheelchair sitting there. On the stairs, Hugo's
phone rings.

DETECTIVE HUGO (OC)
(into phone, increasingly encouraged)
Yes?...Yes...yes...
The Investigator is already at the foot of the stairs in
Eugene's condo when the Detective calls to him.

DETECTIVE
(urgent, to Investigator)
Come quickly. We have him.
The Investigator's eyes light up. He retraces his steps up the staircase after Detective
Hugo.

INT. JEROME'S CONDOMINIUM. DAY.
JEROME, white as a ghost, climbs the stairs, emerging into his own condominium. He
embraces the beaming EUGENE, still sitting on the sofa.

JEROME
(numb)
How are you, Jerome?

EUGENE
Not bad, Jerome.

JEROME
How the hell did you get here.

EUGENE
(deadpan)
I could always walk. I've been faking it.
Jerome almost laughs, despite the situation. Only now does he notice Irene on the other
side of the room, her mind racing.
She looks at Jerome and Eugene together and runs from the apartment.

JEROME
(calling after her)
Irene.
Jerome goes to follow but Eugene stops him.

INT. CRIME LABORATORY. DAY.
An EXTREME CLOSE UP of dried blood - brittle and cracking - on a pair of soiled
latex gloves. A latex head mask, suit of clothes and shoe covers are similarly caked.

The INVESTIGATOR and DETECTIVE HUGO watch as a white-coated FORENSIC TECHNICIAN feeds a minute sample of the dried blood into an analyzer.

The INVESTIGATOR wanders over to a one-way glass window through which he can observe DIRECTOR JOSEF, sitting numb but strangely serene in an interrogation room. The Investigator, in a state of shock himself, cannot yet bring himself to believe what is plainly obvious.

INVESTIGATOR
(gazing at the Director, struggling to come to grips with the turn of events)
This can't be him.

The Detective regards his superior incredulously, intrigued that he could still cling so stubbornly to his theory in the face of such overwhelming evidence.

DETECTIVE HUGO
(intrigued)
We found his spit in the dead director's eye.
He's signed a confession--supplied us with the suit he wore on the night. What more do you want?

INVESTIGATOR
(a trace of desperation, grasping at straws)
Luca could still be an accomplice.

The Investigator turns away, unwilling or unable to accept the explanation. Hugo regards the Investigator with a trace of sympathy. He furtively retrieves the Investigator's tissue from the trash.

INT. GATTACA. DAY.
JEROME sits in a formal briefing room with the other CREW
MEMBERS of his mission, receiving their final pre-flight instructions. LAMAR looks on approvingly.

MISSION COMMANDER
--Finally, I'd like to welcome Navigator Morrow on his debut mission--if we get lost out there, nobody has a map of the heavens in his head like
Jerome.
Jerome looks up bashfully.

MISSION COMMANDER
(adopting a more serious tone)
I'm gratified that there is no longer a cloud hanging over tomorrow's launch. Now we can put this unpleasantness behind us and concentrate on the task at hand. I don't have to tell you how important this mission is--the Belt could hold the key to the origin of life - why we are what we are.
(injecting a note of levity)
I know many of you have been asking that question about me for long enough.
(referring to a projected photograph of a misshapen asteroid behind his head)

Gaspra--how could something so ugly hold so many beautiful secrets?
Polite smiles from his colleagues.

MISSION COMMANDER
Enjoy your final evening with your families.
We'll all be a year older when they see us next. And don't be late tomorrow. You don't
want to miss this.
We focus on Jerome. He appears to have his head in the heavens already.

INT. CRIME LAB. NIGHT.
The tormented INVESTIGATOR lies on the floor of his lab, staring at the ceiling. he
winces in discomfort. He is lying on something. He rolls over and retrieves the irritation
from his pocket. It is the "ESC" computer key he prized from Jerome's keyboard.
He gazes at the key for a moment and then gets to his feet. He resurrects an old
fingerprint kit from a cupboard. Carefully removing the key from the specimen bag -
marked, "MORROW,
Jerome" - he begins to dust it for a fingerprint.
He places the key under a camera. The enlarged print appears on the lefthand side of
his computer screen. The word "MATCH" blinks onto the screen. However the face that
appears from the computer's databank is not that of "MORROW, Jerome" but
"LUCA, Vincent". The Investigator regards the photograph in disbelief.
DETECTIVE HUGO casually enters the lab, something odd in his nonchalant
demeanor.

INVESTIGATOR
(excited)
Hugo! I've found him!

HUGO
I've found him too.

INVESTIGATOR
(not listening, referring to his discovery)
A fingerprint. There's something to be said for nostalgia.
(realizing what Hugo has said)
What did you find?
Hugo puts a specimen bag on the counter. It contains the
Investigator's discarded tissue. The Investigator does not recognize it.

DETECTIVE HUGO
It's not exactly him.

INVESTIGATOR
(interest piqued)
Where did you get this?
The Investigator immediately deposits the tissue into an analyzer.

DETECTIVE HUGO
(referring to the tissue)
But this man does share some common characteristics with your suspect. Not so many but enough. It appears the eyelash has a brother--of a kind.
The Investigator realizes the significance and looks guiltily to Hugo. Hugo exits the lab, leaving the Investigator to stare at his own FACE in his analyzing machine.

INT. GATTACA - JANITOR'S LOCKER ROOM. NIGHT.
CAESAR, the old janitor, enters the locker room. He is about to wearily open his locker when he senses another presence in the room.
He turns to find JEROME sitting there on a bench. Although clearly delighted, CAESAR tries to disguise his pleasure.

CAESAR
So you've finally seen sense and come back to your old job, Vincent.

JEROME
Not yet, I'm afraid.

CAESAR
No? What's keeping you?

JEROME
I guess I'm a slow learner.

CAESAR
I guess so.
(looking up through the small window)
Well, while you're up there, maybe you could tidy the place up a bit.

JEROME
I'll see what I can do.
The two men embrace, Caesar breaking off before Jerome.

CAESAR
And don't go getting everybody lost out there.
You'll give us a bad name. You won't have me to keep an eye on you, you know.

JEROME
(glancing to Caesar's locker)
By the way, I left some trash in your locker.

CAESAR
(happy to oblige)
I'll take care of it.

Jerome departs. Caesar watches him go and turns back to his locker. He opens it to find a brand new, high-tech telescope sitting inside.

The old janitor gets over his surprise and beams broadly - he looks back in Jerome's direction but he has gone. The old janitor cannot help himself and reverently reaches for the telescope's eyepiece.

INT. GATTACA - COMPUTER COMPLEX. NIGHT.

In the dimly-lit, empty computer complex, JEROME takes a last look around. He sits at his computer, one final time replaying the graphic representation of his path through the cosmos that he is on the eve of taking for real.

He notices the key missing from his keyboard. Instantly realizing the significance, he rises from his seat to flee.

INVESTIGATOR
Vincent--

Jerome is stopped in his tracks by the sound of his given name and the voice that calls it.

He makes no further attempt to flee but turns to face his pursuer. The Investigator steps out of the shadows.

INVESTIGATOR
Vincent, what are you running from?

JEROME
(disturbingly calm)
From Vincent.

The two men face each other for the first time in a long time. The Investigator is transfixed by Jerome's face - scarcely able to believe his eyes.

INVESTIGATOR
Has it been so long, you don't remember who I am?

JEROME
(nodding to the Investigator's badge)
Maybe it's you who's forgotten.
(meeting his gaze)
What are you doing here, Anton?

It is finally apparent the Investigator is Jerome's younger brother Anton [AS WE SHALL REFER TO THE INVESTIGATOR FOR THE

REST OF THE FILM].
ANTON
I could ask you the same question.
(glancing to the impressive complex)
I have a right to be here, you don't.

Jerome smiles at him condescendingly.

JEROME
You almost sound like you believe that.

ANTON
(ignoring the remark, extending his hand)
Come with me now, Vincent. You've gone as far as you can go.

JEROME
(refusing Anton's hand, glancing to the telescope above them)
There are a few million miles to go yet.

ANTON
(adamant)
It's over.

JEROME
(shaking his head)
Is that the only way you can succeed, Anton, to see me fail?

ANTON
It's for the best.

JEROME
(increasingly angered)
God, even you want to tell me what I can't do.
In case you hadn't noticed, Anton, I don't need rescuing. But you did, once.
Anton is clearly stung by the memory.

JEROME
(goading)
Well? You have all the answers. How is that possible?

ANTON
(resolute)
You didn't beat me that day. I beat myself.

JEROME
Who are you trying to convince?

ANTON
(angry)
I will prove it to you. Come swim with me now, Vincent. Now--tonight.
Jerome regards Anton with a knowing smile. Somewhere in Gattaca a phone rings.

INT/EXT. IRENE'S CAR OUTSIDE CONDOMINIUM COMPLEX. NIGHT.

IRENE, sitting in her car outside Jerome's condominium, hangs up her portable phone. In her agitation, her finger involuntarily goes to her pulse. She catches herself and removes the finger from her wrist as if it has burned her. She exits the car.

INT. JEROME'S CONDOMINIUM/EUGENE'S CONDOMINIUM. NIGHT.
IRENE quietly knocks on Jerome's door but there is no response.
Trying the handle, the door opens. Her curiosity takes her inside. All is quiet. IRENE calls out.

IRENE
Hello.
No reply. Irene hesitantly ventures further, drawn to the spiral staircase. She tentatively makes her way down the stairs and into Eugene's dimly lit condominium. With wonder and reverence, she examines the instruments and samples laid out on
Eugene's work benches. She opens the refrigerator in the bathroom and inspects the samples and sachets. Finally she regards the empty incinerator.

EUGENE (OC)
Quite something, isn't it?
Irene turns.
Eugene has entered through the mirrored door, not at all displeased by her unexpected visit.

EUGENE
(referring to the incinerator)
That's where we get rid of the traces of him although we never truly succeeded.

IRENE
I've been looking for him. Do you know where he is?

EUGENE
(unconcerned)
He's probably leaving some more of me around the place before he goes.
Eugene idly inspects one of the blood sachets.

EUGENE
Don't be deceived, Irene. These are just the clothes. He has to wear them.
Something I could never do.

IRENE
What's wrong with him?

EUGENE
(sympathetic smile)
You have more in common than you know.
Irene's hand involuntarily goes to her heart.

EUGENE
But they say hisis already ten thousand beats overdue. I have my doubts.
(wry smile)
For all my gifts, they could never engineer me a heart like Vincent's.
Irene turns back to the incinerator, lost in though.

EXT. BEACH. NIGHT.
JEROME and ANTON walk down a dune together towards the beach not far from Gattaca - an ocean beach pounded by an angry, black sea. Jerome picks up a sharp piece of shell and slices the end of his thumb. A drop of blood oozes out. He offers the shell to Anton but Anton does not take it.
Both men begin to disrobe. The brothers stand beside each other on the sand once again - Anton still the more athletically-built of the two.
Together, they enter the raging surf. Diving through the breaking waves, they begin to swim.
In the moonlit night, we watch their two bodies swimming side by side. They swim a long distance, Anton waiting for his brother to tire. But the pace does not slacken. Anton pulls up in the water. Sensing his brother is no longer beside him, Jerome also pulls up. They tread water several yards apart.

ANTON
(attempting to conceal his distress)
How are you doing this, Vincent? How have you done any of this?

JEROME
Now is your chance to find out.
Jerome swims away a second time. Anton is forced to follow once again. Angry now, gritting his teeth, Anton calls upon the same determination we have witnessed during his constant swimming in the pool. He puts on a spurt, slowly reeling in Jerome.
Anton gradually draws alongside Jerome, certain that this effort will demoralize his older brother. But Jerome has been foxing - waiting for him to catch up. Jerome smiles at Anton. With almost a trace of sympathy, he forges ahead again. Anton is forced to go with him. They swim again for a long distance.
It is Anton who gradually becomes demoralized - his strokes weaken, his will draining away. Anton pulls up, exhausted and fearful. Jerome also pulls up. However his face displays none of Anton's anxiety.
They tread water several yards apart. The ocean is choppier now. The view of the lights on the shore is obscured by the peaks of the waves.

ANTON
(panic starting to show)
Vincent, where's the shore? We're too far out.
We have to go back!

JEROME

(calling back)
Too late for that. We're closer to the other side.
Anton looks towards the empty horizon.

ANTON
What other side? How far do you want to go?!
Do you want to drown us both?
(becoming hysterical)
How are we going to get back?!
Jerome merely smiles back at his younger brother, a disturbingly serene smile.

JEROME
(eerily calm)
You wanted to know how I did it. That's how I did it, Anton. I never saved anything for
the swim back.
Anton stares at Jerome, aghast. The two men face each other in silence, treading water
several yards apart in the dark, rolling ocean.
Jerome turns and heads back towards the shore. Anton is left alone with the terrifying
realization. The only sound, the wind and the water.

EXT. CONDOMINIUM. NIGHT.
JEROME, dishevelled and distressed, arrives back at the condominium. He notices
IRENE standing at the edge of the pool.
She turns. He approaches her. They stand several yards apart.
Looking into each other's eyes, they do not speak. Jerome abruptly pulls a hair from his
head - for once one of his own.

JEROME
(wry smile, offering the hair to Irene)
Here, take it.
Irene takes the hair, the significance not lost on her.

JEROME
(echoing Irene's words from their first encounter)
If you're still interested, let me know.
Irene contemplates the hair in her fingers for a moment, then deliberately lets it fall to
the ground.

IRENE
(never taking her eyes from him, echoing
Jerome's words from their first encounter)
Sorry, the wind caught it.
Once again there is not a breath of wind. The hair lies, plainly visible on the edge of the
pool.
From an upstairs window, EUGENE observes the couple.

INT. JEROME'S CONDOMINIUM. NIGHT.
We watch the silhouette of IRENE and JEROME making love in the bedroom.

INT. EUGENE'S CONDOMINIUM. NIGHT.
EUGENE, sitting in his darkened room, unscrews the cap of a plastic container and places it on a nearby table. We remain on Eugene's face as he opens his fly.

INT. JEROME'S CONDOMINIUM. NIGHT.
IRENE and JEROME lie in bed together after making love. For once Jerome is able to sleep unconcerned. It is Irene who lies awake, head against JEROME'S chest, listening to the sound of his erratically beating heart. However it has a soothing effect on her. She kisses Jerome and reluctantly rises from the bed.

JEROME
(awakening)
A year is a long time.

IRENE
Not so long--just once around the sun.
Jerome smiles. For once Irene seems to be looking forward to the trip. She exits the room.

INT. INCINERATOR. MORNING.
Inside the incinerator, JEROME scrapes away at himself - for the final time. He wistfully regards the brush in his hand.

INT. EUGENE'S CONDOMINIUM. MORNING.
JEROME, dressed for his departure, emerges down the spiral staircase into Eugene's condo. Jerome notices several suitcases at the foot of the stairs.
EUGENE wheels into the room.

EUGENE
I have your samples ready.

JEROME
(confused)
Have you forgotten? I don't need any samples where I'm going.

EUGENE
(meeting Jerome's gaze)
No, but you might need them when you get back.
Eugene wheels across the room and opens the mirrored door. The water vapor billows out. Jerome regards Eugene.
Eugene leads Jerome inside for the first time.
Inside are two rows of four identical, industrial refrigerators.
They contain thousands of blood and urine specimens.

Jerome regards them with awe and more than a little unease.

EUGENE
Everything you need to last you two lifetimes.
EUGENE points out an extra specimen of semen in the first refrigerator.

EUGENE
There's an extra specimen. I wish I could give it to her myself.
(afterthought)
But then, you always were better at being me.
Eugene leads the way out of the refrigerator room.

JEROME
(struggling to come to terms with the discovery)
Why have you done this?

EUGENE
(as he seals the mirrored door)
In case you get back before I do.

JEROME
Where are you going?

EUGENE
(glancing to the suitcases)
I'm travelling too.
Jerome goes to question Eugene's travel plans but thinks better of it. He kneels before
his friend and embraces him.

JEROME
Thank you.

EUGENE
I got the better end of the deal. I just lent you my body--you lent me your dream.
Jerome smiles and hugs Eugene a final time. Eugene stuffs an envelope into Jerome's
pocket.

EUGENE
(referring to the note, glancing heavenwards)
Not until you're upstairs.
Jerome exits. Eugene watches him go.

INT. GATTACA - DEPARTURE LOUNGE. NIGHT.
JEROME enters a large holding area along with his other eleven

CREW MEMBERS.

Jerome's heart sinks as he recognizes LAMAR, greeting the crew for one final unexpected substance test. His colleagues groan good-naturedly but it is clearly far more than an inconvenience to Jerome. He looks towards the door he has just entered but there is no way back. One by one the crew are ushered behind a screen. Before he can think of a way out, it is Jerome's turn. He enters the cubicle.

JEROME
(as he takes the plastic cup from Lamar)
What's this, Lamar?

LAMAR
New policy.
From behind, we see Jerome unzip his fly. However for once
Jerome does not urinate on cue - unused to operating his own equipment in front of the physician.

LAMAR
(intrigued by the out-of-character discharge)
Flight got you nervous?

JEROME
There's a problem, Lamar.

LAMAR
(apparently not listening)
Did I ever tell you about my son, Jerome? He's a big fan of yours. He wants to apply here.
Jerome realizes he has no choice. Resigned to his fate, he begins to fill the cup.

JEROME
(as he urinates)
Just remember, Lamar, I could have gone up and back and nobody would have been the wiser--

LAMAR
(cutting him off)
--Unfortunately my son's not all that they promised. But then, who know what he could do.
Lamar takes the cup from Jerome in his gloved hand. Jerome anxiously watches his sample poured into the analyzer.
Confirming Jerome's worst fears, the face of 20-YEAR-OLD VINCENT appears on the computer screen. However Lamar does not look at the screen. He stares Jerome in the eye.

LAMAR
For future reference--

(a brief glance to where
Jerome has just zipped his fly)
--righthanded men don't hold it with their left. It's just one of those things.
Never lookig at the screen, Lamar presses a button marked,

"VALID".
LAMAR
(knowing smile)
Have a safe trip, Vincent.
Jerome exits up a long enclosed escalator, realizing that Lamar has known all along.

INT. EUGENE'S CONDOMINIUM. NIGHT.
EUGENE knocks back a vodka. With a certain reverence he places his silver medal
around his neck.

INT. ESCALATOR. NIGHT.
At the top of a long escalator, the door to a craft is secured.

INT. EUGENE'S CONDOMINIUM. NIGHT.
Eugene's wheelchair, empty, sits beside the door of the incinerator, also secured.

EXT. LAUNCHPAD. NIGHT.
A CLOSE UP of the flame of a rocket's engines igniting - the ball of fire engulfs the
launchpad - filling the screen.

INT. EUGENE'S CONDOMINIUM - INCINERATOR. NIGHT.
Inside the incinerator another ball of fire - this time engulfing the unseen figure of
EUGENE. We glimpse the medal around his neck, melting in the fierce blaze.

EXT. GATTACA - LAUNCHPAD. NIGHT.
As we have seen so often in the past, a rocket launches into the sky over Gattaca -
however on this occasion it carries
Jerome.

INT. SPACECRAFT. NIGHT.
We focus on JEROME's face - seeing little if any of the craft.
Jerome's eyes are closed. His head is still - alarmingly still.
Could the launch itself have been too much for him? He hear the thoguhts in his head.
JEROME (VO)
We came from the stars so they say, now it's time to go back. If I was conceived today,
I would not get beyond eight cells, and yet here I am. In a way they were right, I don't
have the heart for this world.
(pause)
The question is, why am I having so much trouble dying?
Jerome's eyes blink open. He holds the letter from Eugene in his hand. It contains no
words, merely a lock of EUGENE'S hair

- for once preserved solely for its sentimental value. The hair, weightless, floats off the page.
We focus on a porthole looking out upon a starscape.

A STARSCAPE
As we pan across the constellations, a title is superimposed upon the starscape:
In a few short years, scientists will have completed the Human Genome Project, the mapping of all the genes that make up a human being.
After 4 billion years of evolution by the slow and clumsy method of natural selection, we have now evolved to the point where we can direct our own evolution.
The first title is replaced in the heavens by a second title.
If only we had aquired this knowledge sooner, the following people would never have been born:
A succession of portraits and photographs of RENOWNED and
HISTORIC FIGURES fades in and out of the constellations - the accompanying titles list their affliction rather than their accomplishments.

HOMER
Blind from birth

NAPOLEON BONAPARTE
Epileptic

COLETTE
Arthritic

LOU GERHIG
Amyotrophic Lateral Sclerosis
(Lou Gerhig's Disease)

RITA HAYWORTH
Alzheimer's Disease

HELEN KELLER
Blind and deaf

STEPHEN HAWKING
Lou Gerhig's Disease

JACKIE JOYNER-KERSEE
Asthmatic

CHARLES DARWIN
Chronic invalid
The face of Charles Darwin fades off and another title appears out of the stars.

Even Charles Darwin, the man who told of the survival of the fittest, numbered amongst our frailest.

The title fades off and is replaced by one final title in the night sky.

Of course, the other birth that would surely never have taken place is your own.

CUT TO BLACK